D0423175

Joe Johnson

"Preacher, you're the best *pasture* we've ever had!"

Broadman Press/Nashville, Tennessee

To my wife,
Mary Sue,
who has provided
the umbrella during
many a pastoral
cloudburst . . .

© Copyright 1972   •   Broadman Press

All rights reserved

ISBN: 0-8054-2601-9

4226-01

Dewey Decimal Classification Number: 253
Printed in the United States of America

Foreword

As a student of church history, I am always digging around in some old, musty file or outdated book that nobody else cares a thing about. Sometimes I find a treasure that makes all the searching worthwhile—at least to me, if nobody else. One day, while reading the autobiography of a preacher who served churches in Virginia during the early 1800's, I ran across this interesting statement about a problem which he faced at the beginning of his ministry:

> Laughing was deemed, if not sinful, at least quite unbecoming for a Christian, and especially a preacher. . . . Living in a world filled with sin and cursed of God, with thousands passing daily to perdition, it appeared to me most inappropriate that I should indulge in mirth. . . . I resolved to maintain my gravity. For a time I succeeded well. Not a laugh escaped from my lips, and scarcely a smile lighted my countenance. At length, however, some amusing thing was said or done that upset my gravity, and my laughter was all the more convulsive and vociferous because of the long-continued restraint that I had imposed upon it.[1]

To laugh or not to laugh at the experiences of the pastorate seemed to be the problem which this pastor faced. Fortunately, his common sense won out in the struggle. Generations of people were blessed because this pastor was able to admit his humanity by laughing at himself and many of his experiences. Perhaps he discovered the truth which many pastors stumble upon after years of shepherding the flocks of God: A hearty laugh is better than an ulcer any day of the week!

This book of belly-laughs for pastors and laymen by my friend

[1] Jeremiah Bell Jeter, *The Recollections of a Long Life* (Richmond: The Religious Herald Co., 1891), pp. 83-84.

and colleague grew out of his many years experience as a pastor and missionary. I am delighted that I had a small part in bringing the book into being. As editor of *Proclaim,* a magazine of preaching resource materials for pastors, I published an article by Johnson in the October-December 1971 issue of this magazine. Entitled "A Funny Thing Happened on the Way to the Pulpit," this article described the unorthodox method of sermon preparation used by "Lack-o-Preparashun, D.D." The article was designed especially to make the pastor laugh at himself.

Joe Johnson is audiovisual consultant in the Broadman Products Department. Since coming to his present position he has served as supply and interim pastor for churches in the surrounding area.

In this book Johnson has included this essay on sermon preparation as well as other original funny-boners on other aspects of the pastor's work. I recommend the book heartily as an antidote to pomposity and pride—those sins which snap at the heels of us "professional religionists" far more than we like to admit. Blessed is the pastor who knows how to laugh at himself; generations of his parishioners shall rise up and praise his name—long after he has moved on to another church field.

GEORGE W. KNIGHT

CONTENTS

Preamble

Every great document should have a preamble, so here 'tis.

This book defies the laws of hermeneutics, homiletics—and good grammar. And it's person-centered, because it's couched in first, second, and third persons.

If you sit up all night trying to decipher the "message," you're gonna lose a heap of sleep. This tome is written by a preacher to preachers and the "civilians" in the churches. Why "civilians"? Because I cannot abide the unbiblical term, "laity."

Beloved, this volume is not intended for the consumption of twentieth-century Phariseesm Rather, it is tailored for ministers, ordained or unordained, who admit to their humanity. Unless I'm mistaken, the New Testament seems to teach that every Christian is a minister.

WARNING: If you are renowned for your super-piety, bypass this book. But if you're a saint (and every Christian is) with a tarnished halo, and if you enjoy laughter, read on, Macduff.

The mirth contained herein is connected with the most thrilling, and often most frustrating, vocation in the universe—the Christian ministry.

To alleviate your asking, "What did he mean by that?" my aim is very unhomiletical. It has *two* points: (1) to make you chortle, snicker, guffaw, and now and then, break up laughing, and (2) to prod us—I include myself—into taking a sidelong glance at ourselves.

If anywhere in reading this book, you blurt out, "Hey, that guy's talking about me!" remember *you* said it. I refer not only to the "brethren" but to myself. What qualifies me? Nothing except the

Lord has packed 50 years of experiences into my 22 years of preaching.

And I don't attempt to be a respecter of *parsons*—fundamentalist, conservative, liberal, or "constructionist." The preacher who called himself a "constructionist" never did give a definition of himself.

Consider me, although I'm sure you'd rather not. Some call me a fundamentalist. Some call me a conservative. Would you believe there are some who call me a liberal? And there are some who call me *beep-beep*.

Actually, I'm a hyper-liberal fundamentalist, or either a hyper-fundamentalist liberal. And to give you another clue, I'm left-handed. But so is Billy Graham, and so was Leonardo da Vinci. And back where I hail from they had an adage, "The southpaw owes the devil a whole day's work splitting black gum rails." I'm afraid most right handers (the orthodox ones) have labored for Lucifer far more than that!

And to heighten the tone of a scholarly work, you must strive to be a theological "name-dropper." Guys like Harvey Cox—well, you can read them down at the newsstand in a certain popular magazine.

If I dropped the names of some of the people who appear in this book, they would be liable to drop something *on* me, say a ton of bricks. So, names have been changed or omitted to protect the innocent. Who's the innocent? I'm the innocent that I'm trying to protect.

Any similarity between persons living or dead is purely intentional.

JOE JOHNSON

"I was set down in the midst of the valley which was full of funny bones."

— *A Clerical Comedian*

Chapter 1

Prelude to Pastoral Perfection

Years ago I was pastoring so far back in the woods that it required five days for the sunlight to filter through all that chlorophyll.

In one of my primeval churches, perhaps the most faithful attendant was an alcoholic. Back then that dear man was referred to as a "drunk" or a "sot." But he had more sense than most of the other members there, because he never attended when he was sober.

He would sit toward the back, never creating a disturbance although stewed as the proverbial prune. Alas, he was the only person in the congregation with enthusiasm and fire, giving forth with: "Tha's correc', preach'," and "Ar'men." Too bad his fire had to be kindled with fire water.

At the close of the service on a cold, wintry eve, my inebriated member breathed in my face, and *I* became tipsy. Fraternally plopping his arm around my shoulder, he lushly gushed, "You know some'pin, Preacher, you're the best *pasture* we've ever had!"

How was he able to make that penetratingly insightful statement? Why was I "the best pasture" they'd ever had? How can *you* be that caliber of "pasture?"

This volume is devoted to answering that question—once and for all!

*   *   *

Preacher, don't fight it. And civilians, try to understand it. Once a parson's preached, it stays with him, whether he's part-time and works at a secular job, or teaches in college or seminary, or serves in a denominational capacity.

"How can I become unordained?" was the recent question of a reluctant reverend. It's an intriguing question, considering the exodus of ministers from active preaching.

You might as well ask, "Can a tiger shed his stripes?"

There are denominations where untoward ministers are "defrocked" and their credentials are no longer honored. Shucks, in my denomination we never had "frocks" in the first place.

And in certain cases preachers are asked to leave by a congregation or church body. I've had my share of folks who have wanted to "put on the dog," and also put me on the dog, the Greyhound, that is.

Oftentimes when parishioners request a preacher to leave, they're doing him a signal favor. I wouldn't put us preachers in the same breath, but you may recall that many good, religious people insisted that Paul, and even Jesus, vacate the premises.

Paul, do you recollect Lystra, where they stoned you and left you for dead? Jesus, you remember Nazareth, Bethsaida, Chorazin, and Calvary.

But what I'm distressed about is the brethren who not only leave the pastorate, or denominational service, but quit preaching altogether.

Were they mistaken? Was the heat too hot in the kitchen? The reasons, I reckon, are as complicated as our income tax forms. Would more of the brethren survive in the ministry if they could take themselves less seriously?

Man, I've heard about ministerial "dignity" until I'm up to here. One Christian brother was so repulsed by my lack of "dignity" that he suggested I wear a black robe, and then sneak out of the back door of the church when the service concluded.

Preachers who operate like that have a multitude of people who never have the nerve to sneak into their services through any door. Anybody who loves ice that much can travel to the Antarctic or work in a frozen food locker. That "Pomp and Circumstance" ain't my style.

The Pharisees were dignified. They would have put any ecumenical convocation to shame. Contradict me if I'm wrong. But

I simply cannot read "ministerial dignity" into the Lord Jesus.

The dignified rabbis of his day couldn't understand the Nazarene, and didn't care to. Why, he lowered his rabbinic stature by breaking bread with low-down publicans and sinners!

Hey, I want to ask you, "Just how much influence would Jesus have had on the masses if he'd been a pompous stuffed shirt?"

God forbid, though, if we envision our Lord as a "stand up comedian," for that he certainly wasn't, either.

Can't we get just as close to people when we laugh as when we cry? I can't persuade myself that we need more Savonarolas today.

Girolamo Savonarola (1452—98) preached damnation to the lustful citizens of Florence, Italy, and damned they were. He personally spearheaded a campaign of bookburning and a crackdown on vice. The revival was short-lived, and his own people ended up burning Savonarola—at the stake.

I'm not suggesting, though, that you walk around like a hebephrenic, giggling goofily and embarrassing the cause with your inaneness. But can't all of us, whether preachers or laymen, learn to laugh together—not at one another, but with one another?

The minister who is given to laughter is not going to be awarded "Who's Who" in the gallery of the Sanhedrin. But, bless your tickle box, the rank and file will relate to that preacher. Those with the "pruneface perspective" on life are not going to appreciate the cleric who lets out with the "old fashioned" belly laugh.

There's a fine line between laughing and crying for some people. In fact, you've seen folks laugh so hard that they've cried, and cry so hard that they've laughed.

Preacher and layman alike are going to reach more people for the Lord with a smile than a homiletically precise jeremiad from the pulpit.

I'm not calling names, and in this volume no denominations are mentioned. But which churches are growing the fastest in America? Why, the churches that have a free, unstilted, joyful spirit! What's wrong with people who come smiling to Jesus?

Brother, lean back and laugh, uninhibitedly, I heard one preacher criticize another who had referred to a "holy laugh." We need more of 'em. Not critical preachers but holy laughs.

This book (?) is dedicated to the proposition that the greatest revival will be one of joy and laughter. Think of the spiritual revival that would break out if pastors and laymen quit wrinkling the brow and frowning at one another.

The market is inundated with books on how to do everything from clip your toenails to care for a three-toed sloth. And you won't admit it, but you've seen those "everything you wanted to know about . . . " books, usually in paperback.

Here is my offering. You'll never be the same after reading it. One of our "trial readers" should scarcely make it through the "preamble." The last we heard from him, the hospital was giving him "the GI series," and if you don't know what that is, you're neglecting your hospital visitation.

This book should never leave your side. It should be your constant companion. Carry it at all times. One smart aleck suggested that we print it on tissue.

With the book in that form, he could keep it above the sun visor in his car, for emergencies . . . like when his kids throw up after eating out.

This is the most utilitarian little volume you've ever browsed. There's no point in retaining all of those dusty volumes on preaching, church administration, and counseling.

Those old books can furnish considerable warmth during the winter . . . in the fireplace. Beneath *these* covers is the quintessence of ministerial lore and esoteric knowledge.

"Scream loudly and carry a sugar stick."
—*J. Theodore Rapunzel*

Chapter 2

Seven Simple Steps to Sermonic Salubrity

"Kin you preach?" That was probably the first question put to me after I assumed my initial pastorate. After more than two decades, people still have the gall to ask that same question!

In my denomination, the aspiring young preacher is given a "license to preach" by his local church. Upon hearing my first sermon, there were those who wanted to award me a license—a *dog* license.

How could I forget the fright of my first sermon? I was booked to preach at a youth meeting. For four straight weeks folks came by to furnish my transportation to the rally.

I conjured up everything from hives to tularemia to protect myself from being sacrificed to the ecclesiastical wolves. But then the wolves became subdued sheep. When I finally showed up, I preached and preached and preached.

How thrilling—the pastor pulled out a pad and kept notes on my message. Came to find out later that he was trying to figure how to feed and clothe five children on fifty dollars a week (and that was allowing nothing for him and his Mrs.).

One of the "bench members," wiping sleep from his eyes, commented, "Boy, that was some message." I wasn't wild about the inflection in his voice.

At the close of my "licensing" service, and after I had related a minute-by-minute account of my life, one elderly lady prophesied, "Son, you'll be a combination of Peter and Paul." Her prophecy has been gloriously fulfilled. Now I weigh as much as Peter and Paul *combined.*

Listen, I early became accustomed to the fashionable, sophisticated pulpits. During prickly heat season, I have fond memories of one church named after a Greek god (Honest Ionian, I do). The church "plant" was a one-room edifice not far from a swamp. I believe they filmed *The Creature from the Black Lagoon* near there.

It was a sizzling night in mid-July when I stood to sermonize. There was a solitary, naked light bulb right over my head and no screens on the windows.

Every varmint in that swamp was attracted to that light. Orkin had nothing on me. During that sermon, I swallowed more bugs than the average exterminator kills during a week in the spring. And, to boot, a wasp periodically did a whirling dervish on my tongue.

I have in mind another preaching "station." Why do I call it a "station"? Well, because the Wells Fargo came through once a week.

They were worshiping in an abandoned store that had a slit for its only window. The temperature was about 105 degrees in the shade, and hotter inside. The children and two or three of the adults were barefooted, so I decided to join them.

You'd have thought I was Clark Kent in a phone booth. Off with the coat, off with the tie, off with the shirt, and off with the socks and shoes. In case you're morally outraged, I finished my act—er, sermon—in thick tee shirt and trousers.

While a ministerial student, I journeyed out to another station which was meeting in a home. Upon my return, my mother[1] asked me, "Son, how did it go?" I replied, "Mom, we had 106 present."

Mom exulted, "Why, that's wonderful, son." To which I responded, "Yep, 106— six human beings and 100 baby chicks." Verily, those gospel birds drowned out my message. Since that time I've carried on a personal vendetta against all grown chickens. I've devoured as many of them as possible.

In my denomination, if a licensed preacher "proves" himself, his church then proceeds to ordain him, usually after he has hornswoggled a church into calling him. After being on trial longer

---

[1] She's the *evangelist* who led me to Jesus.

than Sacco and Vanzetti, I was called to a church.

Among the elements of my ordination service, I remember the advice of an 83-year-old preacher who was still going strong.[2] His voice cracked and wheezed as he challenged, "Be sweet." I'm sure that many of my members have called me "saccharin." I've been too sweet and turned bitter.

You may contend that this chapter is bypassing the "Big B's"—Broadus, Blackwood, and Buttrick. However, if you'll masticate the flavorful filling of this chapter, people will no longer inquire of you, "Can you preach?"

They'll KNOW . . .

. . . . . you can't!

*   *   *

Through the years I have read many articles by famous preachers on "How I Prepare My Sermons." These preachers have diversified methods. They approach the subject from every direction.[3]

One prominent pulpiteer testified that he writes his sermon ideas on 3 by 5 cards and stuffs them into a desk drawer. Then, from time to time, he shuffles through these ideas and culls the stack.

Another preacher uses the "moral rearmament" approach, which is valid in certain situations, I suppose. He selects his sermon topics by designating a certain day in the week as "sermon selection day." The following Sunday he preaches on the first thing that had come to mind on "sermon selection day." That sort of fell through after a while, though, because one morning his first thought was about a septic tank!

And I hear tell that one fellow in my native region selected his text like this. The mattress on his bed was extremely bouncy, so he would pitch his Bible onto the bed until it (the Bible, not the bed) fell open. He would then choose his text from one of the two exposed pages.

Now I've said all that to say this: My method of sermon

---

[2]When he later passed away, he was engaged to marry a fifty-year-old lady the next week.

[3]From *Proclaim*, Oct.-Dec. 1971. ©Copyright 1971, The Sunday School Board of the Southern Baptist Convention. All rights reserved. Used by permission.

preparation is effortless and uncluttered. Why even bother writing ideas on file cards? I write 'em on menus, pink stationery, napkins, paper tablecloths, backs of torn football tickets—you name it. Inspiration's the thing!

And I'm not too concerned about putting my ideas into a desk drawer. I have a most serviceable filing system. I stash these ideas and "sermon starters" in the glove compartment of the car, behind the sun visors, in the refrigerator, and now and then, in a place where I can actually locate them! One of the best sermons I ever preached came from the box in which my wife stores her hair dryer.

I simply cannot understand these preachers who claim they sweat over a sermon. You know, those brethren who say how long it requires them to develop an idea, nurse it along, rough it out, and then develop a polished sermon.

Why, I remember the old boy who was in college with me. As a mere kid he had a church, and I was one of the "have not's" at the time. It thrilled me when he piously asserted, "The longest I ever spend preparing a sermon is ten or fifteen minutes at the most!" That made a tremendous impression upon my young mind. I thought that was fantastic. Come to think of it, though, he's not preaching anymore!

Now then, how do I put that sermon into shape after I've gotten the idea? Do I go to my files? Do I gather material from different sources? Nope.

Here's my approach. Sometime late Saturday afternoon I systematically gather my sermonic bits and pieces. A piece of facial tissue, on which my wife has blotted her lips, has scrawled on it a gem of alliteration—three cohesive points which serve as the launching pad for Sunday morning's pulpit blast-off.

"Sin, Satan, and Salvation." Doesn't that have a ring to it? But there are some alternate words which I manage to ferret from behind the refrigerator. How does "Soup, Society, and Syncretism" sound? I don't have the slightest idea what that last word means, but it sure sounds good!

I'm on my way, at least for Sunday morning, and I have time aplenty. By now it's only 8:30 on Saturday night. I always work better under pressure. These ideas require a freshness that comes only with spontaneity. What else now? Concordances? Greek New Testament? Lexicons? Commentaries? By this time it's time for coffee and the Saturday night movie on TV.

All the while, my basic points are fermenting and ruminating in my brain. I'm building my points as I'm sipping coffee, eating cold cuts, and watching, "Godzilla Meets the Wolf Man, Frankenstein, and Tonto." "The Seriousness of Sin," "The Slyness of Satan," and "The Sufficiency of Salvation." See there!

Notice my progress in preparation. It's now 10:30 and Godzilla, Wolf Man, Frankenstein, and Tonto have sauntered into the East (not the West).

All I need now is to put meat on these study bones of my sermon. So off I go to my study and very methodically stack up my references. These consist of two books of sermon illustrations. One is entitled, "One Thousand Nine Hundred and Fifty of My Favorite Deathbed Stories," and the other is called "Compendium of Selected Illustrations for Clubs, Civic Organizations, Luncheons, After-dinner Speeches, Locker Rooms, and Every Occasion." That one is the abridged edition.

With these illustration books I've assembled Spurgeon, Truett, Torrey, Moody, and J. Frank Freebie. Who's Freebie? I don't have the foggiest notion, but I got a good deal on his book. I bought it for fifty cents at the Salvation Army Thrift Store.

This is where the travail of soul appears, the marshaling of all my redeemed powers! How shall I adapt these brethren to my sermon? It's pretty difficult with Spurgeon, who uses phrases like "lay it to heart," "fearful disposition," etc. But even those outdated phrases have a good ring to them.

Now I have my three points. Every point is fortified with these great pulpit giants. Every point is buttressed with at least one tearjerking story. Write it out? Manuscript? What, do you think I would dare limit divine leadership?

I will carry those three points into the pulpit with me, written either on my cuff (that's why I don't wear those stylish colored shirts into the pulpit) or on the back of a green stamp book. Do I at least write out the introduction and conclusion? Naw! I like to let nature take its course. Kinda play it by ear.

If the congregation lags, I have a file of jokes (from Joe Miller on down) tucked in my cranium. To impress the folks with my learning and scholarship, I have certain words at my fingertips, like "relevant," "precious," "bless your heart," "Mama," and "dearly beloved."

When you put as much into it as I do, preaching is a sheer joy!

What will I do about Sunday night? You guessed it. I do most of that preparation while watching pro football on Sunday afternoon. Where can you find better illustrations than in the manly game of fooball? You know, "the game of life," "teamwork," "don't fumble the ball. . . ."

"Through your services, your parishioners should be ushered into the presence of a higher power—the TV ratings of your morning service."

—*Helmut Thickly*

Chapter 3

The Misconduct of Services

I overheard this conversation only last week. Because I'm a snoop, I'll share it with you.

Bob: Hey, we're really groovin'. We're gonna lay it on 'em, if Barry doesn't cop out. We can't hit the scene without our dobro player.

Janet: Right on. Outta sight. I'm zapped by Barry's playing. He's heavy. But what about Joe Joe?

Bob: Oh, wow, Joe Joe's heavy, too. I'm worried, though. Joe Joe's out cruisin'—trying to replace his busted sitar strings. Bird baby, we're gonna bomb out if we have a dead dobro and a sick sitar.

Janet: Like yeah. Does Hubie have the black light laid out? That black light just freaks me out.[1]

Dear reader, you have already gathered that I eavesdropped on two "hippies" plotting a way-out rock festival, complete with liquor and drugs. Right? Wrong! That was Janet Klop and Bob Foist discussing plans for a Sunday service in their tradition-bound old church. Janet and Bob are grandparents several times over; Janet grooves—er—plays lead guitar, and Bob hits a heavy tambourine.

Surely you haven't exclaimed, "What's the world coming to?" Oh, wow, you oughtta lay your ocular orbs on that church's youth group. They're the heaviest, coolest, and grooviest!

[1]Translation: Bob and Janet are discussing the upcoming performance of their band. They are thrilled by the playing of Barry and Joe Joe. They, however, are apprehensive concerning Barry's participation. Joe Joe is diligently seeking replacement strings for his instrument. Their band's performance will prove a failure without the complement of dobro and sitar, and the special lighting effects. Due to changes in vernacular, "Groovin'," "cop out," "Right on," "hit the scene," "Outta sight," "zapped," "Bird baby," "bomb out," and "freaks me out" will probably be passe by the time this reaches you.

Brethren, I've heard that only *8* percent of church members *enter* a church because of the preacher. But isn't it strange that *80* percent claim to *exit* on account of him.

Preach, you gotta plug in, tune in, and turn on. And you have to keep on generating the ecclesiastical electricity.

Most of your members and prospects are entertainment conscious. "All the world's a stage." Even though you've heard that pro football is the number one spectator sport, don't believe it. The game at church has that distinction.

They can turn off the radio or television, but they can more easily turn *you* off by staying away. If only you could envision yourself as the ringmaster, what an exhilarating difference it would make in your services.

Really, your ministerial association should conduct a poll to gauge the rating of churches in your community.

You'll discover that the churches in the "Top Ten" have these characteristics in common: they have a "tuned in" preacher who majors in comedy, and a constant procession of variety acts that would make Ed Sullivan jealous.

Forty years ago the radio was the "devil's box." Twenty-plus years ago television was lambasted as "hellevision." In evangelical churches, dancing has often been suspect. But in some churches where dancing has been taboo, now (to quote that sensitive poet), "There's a whole lotta shakin' goin' on."

Praise the Lord that the essence of the gospel doesn't change! But as you read this, our methods of presentation will be altering like a chameleon on a piece of polka dot material.

When I entered the ministry, my approach to worship services was low key. Although gifted with a double portion of tomfoolery, I saved the jocularites for the church suppers and "dinners-on-the-ground." I wanted to strike a "happy medium" (if I ever saw a "happy medium," I wouldn't strike him—I may not agree with his doctrine, but I'm not gonna resort to violence).

My conduct of services was not bad, considering the accolades I received. From one saint I heard the same appraisal every Sunday, "I enjoyed your talk—both of them." He never called them sermons.

And from another member, "It was real." And another, "Preacher, if you hold out much longer, I'm gonna bring a 'cold 'tater'."

Yes, I aimed for a service which combined good taste and at least a scintilla of reverence. Judged by Nielson, though, my services would have been preempted and finally cancelled. Why, all we did was pray, welcome the people, make the announcements, sing hymns, read the Bible, receive the offering, preach the sermon, and give the invitation. Blah.

And I preached with gusto. The Lord gave me a barrel for a chest and a bellows for lungs. The folks heard my messages. Maybe that was the trouble. Whether they heeded is another matter. The elderly gent I baptized when he was eighty-eight testified that I was the only preacher he'd been able to hear in thirty years.

There I was, visiting the sick, conducting weddings, burying the dead, baptizing my share of folks (and hopefully a goodly percentage of my candidates were saved). You know, I was performing those "straight, square" functions that we used to associate with "ministry."

It was strongly suggested that we have a visiting preacher (kin to some of the members) for a revival meeting. I'd neither met him nor heard him preach.

My spouse should be teaching homiletics in the seminary. When my pulpit offerings are odoriferous, Mary Sue does not spray them with an aerosol can. I had to agree with the Mrs. that said guest preacher was a "tense" sermonizer. He stink, stank, stunk in any tense. Forgive my grammar.

He preached the kind of sermons that last you a lifetime. You wanted to forget them, but you couldn't. They clung like the vapor trail of a Central Tennessee polecat.

Every preacher's heard the punch line, "Weak point here. Scream like you-know-where." Our visitor must've felt that every one of his points was weak. He screamed and wailed like a "meemie."

He not only punctured eardrums: Beloved, the cars in the parking lot had blowouts! And his pyrotechnics were not restricted to vocal effects. His arms reminded me of cobras tangling with mongooses (or is it geese?).

You'd have thought the church was having an indoor tennis match, as that pulpit incendiary ran footraces with the devil.

In a word, we thought he was horrendous.

After a period of convalescence, I paid a call on one of "Rev. Perpetual Motion's" relatives.

"Isn't_____a wonderful preacher?" she asked, snuff juice gurgling. I tried not to answer.

"You know something, preacher. Maybe after you've been preaching another ten or fifteen years, you'll be able to preach half as good as him."

The sound that echoed in the valley was yours truly falling out of the wicker chair. Thus began my ministerial metamorphosis.

Yes sir, the preacher is the "parson." THE PERSON. In the church service he not only has the center of attraction (unless his church has a split chancel), he must labor to maintain it. This is why so many preachers are going into movies and television.

I sure wish I could retake a stack of my pulpit clinkers, especially when my teeth were being worked on and I pronounced r's like l's and vice versa. And when I've called people by the wrong names. And like when I publicly recognized Mr. and Mrs. _____, and discovered after the service that Mr. and Mrs. weren't married, or even engaged.

And like when I unintentionally transposed the letters of two words, to my beet-redness, and was thankful that the only one listening was an understanding teen-ager.

"Variety is the spice of life," and from the vicissitudes of life, I have learned to conduct the spiciest services around.

There are planned and unplanned services, structured and unstructured services, but the preacher in command will *plan for unplanned services.* Now that requires ingenuity. (Compare chapter 4—"The Braille System of Church Administration.")

Like the pro quarterback, you must have a game plan. You map out the method of handling the opposition. In your case that's the devil and his cohorts. When the devil's linebackers start "blitzing," you become a scrambling quarterback. And most of the brethren have to scramble like "Crazy Legs."

Recently I perused a magazine which was devoted to "the black church." One premise of the issue was: through the years black people have rejoiced in the "freedom" of their preachers. If a black minister has a "following," his folks'll do what he wants.

Unfortunately, I'm handicapped, I'm a Scotch-Irish, German WASP.

When his members accuse a black preacher of preaching "white," that's considered an insult. As one black brother observed, "You people keep the Lord locked up and hedged in. Let him loose." Amen!

Seminary libraries are bulging with musty volumes on "pulpit decorum," "ministerial dignity," and programed worship. Most of us are taught that the Lord can't move after 12 o'clock noon on Sunday. At 12:01 P.M. water skiing and pot roast have precedence.

Yes, we pulpiteers have learned to be polished and smooth. One preacher was so smooth that he reminded his listeners of clean bed sheets. He put 'em to sleep.

If you remember nothing else, carve this on your desk. Structure your services to be unstructured! Print your bulletins with ample white space. Your sermon samplers, spellbound with your messages, can transcribe your unprepared, unstructured outlines.

In between Sunday School and the morning service, call your team in for that last-minute huddle. The lights and camera are ready. All that remains is the action. Because of your spontaneous, unstructured services, the gathering congregation is as quiet as a bull fight in Barcelona.

Shades of Knute Rockne and Vince Lombardi. "All right, gang," you intone, hands on hips. "This is the Super Bowl. It's winner take all. What you do out there will reflect on the character of our team. Alma, are you willing to pull out all the stops?"

"Yeah, Coach," shrieks Alma, with upraised fist. Alma is your 88-pound organist responsible for "kicking off" the game.

"Where's Beatrice," you inquire of Alma. Beatice Gripper is your pianist.

"Coach, she was unable to suit up. She's injured with two infected hangnails."

The team pauses for a moment of silence. You remember Beatrice Gripper.

"Freddie, you will recall that your 'end-around' almost lost the game for us last time out. Make it an 'end sweep' this time. Hear?"

"I hear you loud and clear, Coach."

Freddie, your minister of education, had bumped you behind the pulpit and nearly knocked you into the potted chrysanthemums. He was reacting more like a corner back with the Kansas City Chiefs.

"George, the team spirit is lagging. You'll have to raise the spectators to a higher peak." George, sometimes called music director, is head cheer leader.

"Coach, we have a problem seating the fans," observes Harry, the head usher. Harry reports that most of the fans want a seat on the fifty-yard line.

"What's wrong with that?"

Harry replies, "Nothing, except all of them want to start *sitting ten rows back.*"

Now the band has struck up your fight song. Rather, Alma is playing "Three Cheers for Old Central Church." Harry is on the "field" striving to seat 100 fans on the tenth row at the fifty-yard line.

You, Freddie, and George, keyed-up for the fray, are ready to spring onto the field. The three of you clasp hands, and it reminds you of boyhood when you chose up sides for "hard" ball. Grim determination is etched in your faces.

Gazing with knowing looks first at Freddie and then at George, the cry leaps from your throat, "Let's go out there and win this one for the Gripper!"

What uniforms will your team wear? The first requisite, of course, is clothes. Most choir's cheerleaders wear robes, but what about clerical vestments for the minister. (I belong to a denomination in which a purplish-blue suit was once the standard "habit.")

I have knowledge of a denominational brother who pioneered in clerical garb. His sermons on damnation were unusually vivid, since he pastored an air conditionless church in Nevada. His vestments consisted of a long black robe, and nothing beneath but a false shirt front and his swim trunks!

Brethren, I admonish you to dress tastefully. One of my preacher friends has exceedingly tasteful attire. His ties and shirts are full of gravy, eggs, and coffee.

If you lack confidence in your preaching, wear outlandish clothes, and the zanier the better. When you don Mafia sunglasses indoors, a vermillion shirt, and fuchsia tie, fire-engine-red trousers, and patriotic shoes, they're not going to hear your sermon anyway.

Atmosphere is not what surrounds the earth. It's what you have to simulate and stimulate in your church services. You and the church leadership must consider the comfort of the congregation. That's why concrete-hard pews are advisable. Under—rather—over those circumstances, your members will find it difficult to catch four winks.

Have "fast tracks" installed in the aisles. This will facilitate your sermonic excursions into the crowd and also double your public decisions.

If the sanctuary has windows, stain 'em the color of pitch, thereby eliminating outside distractions from "fauna." I can make this statement without fear of contradiction: dogs, cats, and other fauna are naturally attracted to my preaching.

In one church I was giving the evangelistic invitation, and a "blue tick" hound answered the call, came down the center aisle, and stood by me. I'm glad he was house-broken. Another time I was on my knees, with eyes closed, in a country prayer meeting. A sudden wetness flicked across my face. Thinking the flick was a snake, I later rejoiced to learn that it was "Ebony," my dog, giving me a facial.

At another church, "Quilty," our feline, made her public commitment. And I remarked, half-truthfully, "This cat has more sense than half the people in this community."

I'm not entering into this "kids say the funniest things" bit, but they do. And they can *do* some not-so-funny-things, too!

I've pastored more than one church where there's a steady procession of kids availing themselves of the church's water-related facilities. I suggested to a certain music director that we consider having five or six interludes, complete with "Pomp and Circumstance" and the processional from "Aida," during every service. Half of that church's budget was dedicated to the water bill.

So help me, this happened to a friend of mine. He was presenting the invitation at the close of the service. A teen-age girl pushed into the aisle and sauntered toward my friend.

With unbridled joy, he met her five giant steps up the aisle. Clasping her hand, he emotionally asked, "My dear, why do you come today?"

She tersely replied, "Preacher, would you please let me by. I gotta use the rest room."

Yes, your parishioners must have comfort and convenience. In the dead of winter, our church auditorium reminded one of the Kalahari Desert. The members broke out in a sweat. At first I thought my dynamic preaching had them under conviction.

Men shucked their coats and pulled off their ties. Women fanned furiously with the denominational papers. More than once we found the thermostat set on 92 degrees. One cold-natured couple had insisted on broiling the brethren. The board considered stationing a guard by the controls.

In a congregation where I was visiting preacher, one woman had an aversion to the church's air conditioning. That sensitive soul, bless her allergies, helped the rest of the membership "sweat off those ugly pounds" every summer.

A few of your members are liable to have a fixation about time, like the church which had a giant clock behind the pulpit. I preached a revival meeting there. Some people had lovingly remarked, "Your face would stop Big Ben." I was wishing that my mug would stop that clock.

In tender love, of course, I publicly suggested that the ladies sew a drape to place over it. Would you believe that those "sweet thangs" (sic) threatened to sew a burial shroud for yours truly?

One old song goes, "I have no record now of time." You

shouldn't, either. If the natives become restless, exhort all the longer. "Finally," "In conclusion," "Moreover," "At last," and "I close with this" will help your congregation see that you're going to quit someday, "in the sweet by and by."

Now, gentle people, we will broach the subject of the elements of the service. While the congregation is engaged in what you call preliminaries (you know, singing, special music, etc.), no one can forget for a moment your presence.

Always assume that your music director has laryngitis, and therefore his vocal deficiency must be overcome by your mellifluous voice. Complement the service by individually bellowing more gustily than the Cossack Choir. And like the raw recruit whose mother thought was the only GI in step, deliberately sing a half-beat off. Then, the music director, choir, and the entire congregation will realize they're wrong.

And when you're presiding, and the minister of music and/or education are having their half-minute's worth, it's your duty to give them moral encouragement. Afford them a steady background of hearty "amens" and "that's right" and "praise the Lord." Your piety, not to mention your humility and politeness, will leave a profound impression upon your people.

And when you're in the driver's seat, keep your staff on its toes. While a thousand eyes are upon him, ask the educational director, "Freddie, how are plans for the retreat coming along?"

With flushed face, Freddie chokingly stammers, "Uh—er—uh—what retreat?"

To which you reply, "That's OK, Freddie boy. If you had good sense, you'd be dangerous. Ha! Ha!" The worshipers are musing, "How stupid of Freddie." Of course, they don't know that you intended to discuss the matter of the retreat with Freedie three months ago, but—well, you were excruciatingly busy.

Anyway, every church ought to have staff members with ESP.

And any minister worth his salt will sustain the repartee. Single out members of the congregation for special recognition, either during your welcome, announcements, or sermon.

"Hey, Charlie Drubnik, we heard about your-hole-in-one. All of us were curious where you were during Sunday School last week. Chuckle!"

"It's favorite hymn time, folks. All of you know Ima Loner, one of our precious old maids." (Ima's only 27.) Ima's favorite "hims" are him *(pointing)*, and him, and him. Heh!

"Beloved, I have above sin. That's correct. At Pious Polytechnic I lived on the second floor of the men's dorm, and Floyd Floogle's room was directly below mine. Right, Floyd? Ho! Ho!"

A pivotal element of the service is the offering. Black preachers have confidence in their sermonizing, because most of them "lift the offering" after the sermon. I heard of a Scotch preacher who tried that once, and once was enough. His members made him pay!

And I heard tell of a brother who almost starved after he announced, half-jestingly, "No cash, please—only large checks." There's an art to lifting the offering. One friend of mine has attended more than his share of those campaigns where those deep, noisy, plastic buckets are used. His ushers have gone one better—they're using deep, noisy, metal trash cans. You can scarcely hear the rustle of bills, but oh, you kid, those coins!

The people must become involved, not only in reading responsively and singing the hymns. Have dialogue periods. Preach, instead of performing your usual stand-up monologue, sit down on one of those uncomfortable stools that TV guitar pickers use.

"Rap" with your people. Let them talk back for a change. One of my ministerial mateys experimented with that dialogue deal. His members "rapped" him so hard that his noble experiment expired. It was merely that some of his members had been trying to communicate with him for months. Rapping had unclogged the lines.

And nothing can unhinge a service more than encouraging personal testimonies. Now testimonies are being utilized even by formal, liturgical churches.

Blessed a thousand-fold is the pastor who has loquacious testifiers. They will help you have a homiletical holiday.

Once I called on a young preacher to give "a five minute testimony of what Jesus means to you." Jesus meant an hour's worth to him!

What a relief! It was a twofold blessing. I was given a rest, and my members heard a new voice.

Another interesting wrinkle is innovative prayer. Once upon a meeting, I requested that several laymen lead our congregation in sentence prayers. You'd have thought they were *life* sentences.

Our denomination has over 2500 foreign missionaries serving in 80 countries. One of those missions-minded brethren, in his sentence prayer, remembered 78 of those countries—by name. He must've been tired. He missed Chad and Sierra Leone!

Hear me, brothers of the cloth, if you're going to have vibrant services, if you're going to involve the people, if you're going to allow creativity, sell your watches and donate the moolah to the Internal Revenue.

If everybody gets into the act, your folks'll never make it to work on Monday morning, and you won't make it to the lake for fishing. Monday is your day off, I hasten to add.

On the other hand, though, you can emulate the example of a few industrious brethren. They should be addressed as "Father," because they believe in religion by proxy. They do it all, double in brass!

They preside, make all of the announcements, direct the music, sing the specials, lead in every public prayer, and preach. This method not only magnifies the minister by allowing for ample display of his variegated talents, but perpetuates the apa—er—tranquility of the members.

Finally, brethren . . . I was preaching a revival meeting in a country church (haven't preached too many elsewhere) and waxing eloquent, enchanted by my voice. As I developed point seven, a first-grade boy blurted out, "Mama, why doesn't that fat man sit down, and shut up and let the pastor preach?" Point seven evaporated.

Although I'd rather not, I can recall pastoring a small-town church while I was a student in the seminary. One Sunday was especially trying, and at the close of the evening service a certain lady, who wasn't enamoured with me, declared out loud, "Two more sermons like I've heard today, and I'm leaving this church."

The following week I was offered five bribes to preach exactly the same two sermons the next Sunday. I had to turn them down, because—for the life of me— I couldn't remember my own sermons!

"This' the way I run the church,
Run the church,
Run the church."
—*J. Frank Moot*

Chapter 4
The Braille System of Church Administration

This is the era of the programers. Maybe the stamp in the forehead is not far away. They've given you a number, and taken 'way your name, to paraphrase an r & r song.

Everything must move with computerized mechanization. Take the Federal Government, for instance. Oh, you don't want it? Yes, in the Federal Government, everything is "programized." That marvelous programing, at this writing, is leading our nation to a debt of nearly 500 billion dollars. Man, wouldn't it be wonderful if our churches could spend money that way and get by with it.

So, we have to gird up our loins for programing, And I'm all agreed with it. There's nothing like being prepared.

Several of my compatriots have attended those church administration clinics or seminars. There they've learned about every phase of administering a church program.

They've become geared to church development, which extends over a year; medium-range for two years; and long-range planning for five years or more. Can you imagine that? I have trouble planning to climb out of the bathtub!

That planning stuff is okay for them. Those fellows contend that there are benefits to planning far ahead. In fact, one cleric declared that he had planned his ministry twenty-five years ahead of time. He would serve as pastor until a ripe-young age and then retire with a certain number of benefits. Marvy, isn't it? He must not be planning to serve some of the places I have.

I have experimented with all shades of planning, believe me. One renowned clergyman was heard to expostulate, "Brethren, in the ministry, you must think ahead. You must outguess your

parishioners. If necessary, arise at 4 A. M. to stay ahead of them."
Sad, but some of his members had insomnia. They were up *all night long* doing their planning.

Back when I started preaching (and it wasn't that long ago), our philosophy of church administration was, "Play it by ear." That was a favorite expression of a layman in one of my churches. I tried it. It sounded superb, except I developed a cauliflower ear.

Another jewel of advice was, "Hang loose." I tried that. I was hanging so loose, my members began calling me "Toulouse" (for Lautrec). Well, needless to note, I quit hanging so loose when several of my parishioners decided to tighten up.

After my exposure to church administration, I decided to seek its definition in the dictionary. Administration is defined as The performance of the executive duties of an institution, business, or the like. It's also referred to as, in a narrower sense, the activity of the executive and judiciary departments, or especially of the executive alone in the conduct of government.

When I read that last phrase, I began to warm up to this administration bit. Yum, yum, "the activity of the executive alone." And isn't the pastor an executive?

I started to read again. The dictionary continued, "The management and disposal, under legal authority, of the estate of a deceased person, or of an infant, lunatic, etc." Brother, that last phrase grabbed me. In one paragraph I'd gone from an executive to a lunatic!

Anyway, church administration is the process of carrying on the ministry and work of the church. Hark, all ye administrators. The paramount and peerless principles which I present for your perusal are part and parcel of painstaking pastoral pedantry.

The first maxim of administration is: keep the congregation in suspense. I'm built like Alfred Hitchcock, anyhow, so that's rather easy.

Why worry the membership with the details of what's going on in the church? Isn't that why the church has a *pastor* and *board* (or whatchamacallit), or deacons, or stewards, or elders, or vestry, *u pluribus unum?*

In fact, brother minister, since *you* are the executive officer, why not let the church leadership rest, too? They'll adore you for it. Now I would not want you to read me wrong. Planning and programing are necessary adjuncts to a smoothly-oiled ecclesiastical machinery. But too many mechanics gum up the works. And too many cooks spoil the broth. Preacher, among the cooks, you are Chef Boy Ardee.

Because of my superabundance of modesty, I shall not dwell on my c. a. achievements. Rather, let me refer you to the programing of a co-picker in the vineyard, the Rev. E. Z. That's a *non de plume,* because his members are still trying to reach him since his resignation.

Of the "ear players" and "hangers loose," he *was* the epitome. Then, he lost his derring-do and became enamoured with precise programing. He actually started planning more than three days ahead of time.

It was the beginning of the ending for Rev. E. Z. Prior to his disappearance, he and the church secretary had labored long and hard on the mimeographed church calendars for the upcoming year. Mountains of crisp paper were piled high. Brother E. Z. stepped back and smacked his lips. All was in readiness.

There was an air of expectancy. And there was *another* air. The church custodian had a stopped-up nose, opened wide the windows to the hall, and admitted a thirty-five-mile-an-hour wind.

They're still picking up Brother E. Z.'s carefully-programed year as far away as Saskatoon, Saskatchewan.

Maybe proxy religion is not so bad after all. Let the *officials* administer the program. Could I share a heart-throbbing testimony with you? The man's name is withheld to avoid undue embarrassment to his immediate relations.

"My name is *blip.* Under our former pastor, there was anxiety and worry among the members. But no more. We used to be bothered with nonessentials like voting on building programs, church budgets, calendars of activities, and salaries for the staff. But now, think of the relief. No more committee meetings, and maybe business sessions once a year.

And there is terrific excitement in our congregation, because we never know what's going to happen. Now, going to church is similar to reaching in a grab bag. There's just no telling—chuckle—what cute innovation our pastor, Reverend *tweet* will come up with. Hee! Hee!"

Be careful as you lead him away there. That's right.

Did you hear the salient points of his testimonial? There is "terrific excitement" in his congregation. The people have such enjoyment.

In *blip's* church the families play games as they ride to church. They also ask questions.

Like: "I wonder what special day we're going to observe?"

"What kind of literature will we be studying in Sunday School today?"

"What will happen in the worship service?"

"Will we have a dialogue sermon, no sermon at all, congregational choreography, or will Pastor *beep* disguise himself as John the Baptist sans head?"

"Will Pastor *beep* preach Christmas, Easter, New Year's, Father's Day, Mother's Day, National Pickle Week, or Be Kind to Humans Week sermons?"

"Or, better still, will he mix all of them together and call his message a "tutti frutti testimony?"

The cardinal rule, I reiterate, is keep 'em guessing. Number two is: rely on your intuition. Call it inspiration, if you will. Size up the situation and "get the hang" of it.

The intuitive method still leaves room for planning, but also provides elasticity. There are three methods of intuitive planning.

Short-range. . . . There is no substitue for this method. Beloved, in this approach you never fire until you see the "reds" of their eyes.

This form of planning occurs while you are on your feet behind the pulpit. There you speak *ex cathedra.* "Brethren, we ought to initiate this program because it's just now been laid on my heart."

If a soul dare question your impromptu program, question his spirituality. With this method, Willikers, think of all the straining and sweating you've saved the congregation. Besides, you can always remind yourself that this new program has been brewing for twenty years.

There is no problem in implementing this type of programing, either, because you'll have to do it all yourself! What a saving! No boring committee meetings, no infernal questions and answers, no accounting, and no guff. Oh, I might add that there are times when intuitive planning can be done while you're sitting on the platform. But it's much more creative on your feet, since the brain can be exercised.

Next, there is medium-range intuition. Most ministerial planners fall into this broad spectrum. I never saw a broad spectrum, and hope that I never do.

Medium-range is planning at least *three* to *five days* ahead of time. I've always heard the expression, "Informed people are happy people." Being informed of budget campaigns, revival meetings, and building programs three to five days ahead of time will call for less faith on the part of your members, of course. There's still no substitute for the short-range method.

Another definite drawback to medium-range projection is this: an advance notice gives the members time to brood, and possibly worry, about the outcome of the program. But remember, there are different levels of motivation. You must meet your people where they are. Overnight, you cannot expect them to be spiritual enough to fully appreciate the insight of your short-range approach.

Admittedly, then, medium-range planning leaves much to be desired, and it's three to five days worse than nothing. It'll naturally require more advance planning on your part. But shouldn't you stay on your toes? And it's far less complicated now, since most evangelical churches have lifted the ban on ballet.

The least desirable method is long-range programing. Preachers who indulge in this approach do not have sufficient confidence in the unswerving faith and loyalty of their parishioners. All of this planning and programing can undermine the sweet paternal relationship which exists between shepherd and flock, spiritual father and children, king and subjects.

Blush! This long-range approach means that the administrator must plan at least ten days to two weeks in advance! Consider the fretting and fussing your members can do in that length of time. Remember, Hank Williams, Sr. and Henry Mancini wrote several of their top songs in thirty minutes or less.

Long-range can become exhorbitantly expensive, too. If your members are budget-conscious, they want to save money, don't they? Why, with this method you might have to buy calendars, mimeograph paper, and poster board. Do you recognize now how complicated this unspiritual method can become?

And with this long-range tack, you might have to conduct planning meetings. To quote one of my all-time favorite leaders, "Preacher, whatever you decide to do, I'm for it." Now there's a man after a pastor's own heart. May his tribe increase—to more than 144,000 descendents, I trust.

A perennial committee member once observed, "Whew, in the 20 years I've belonged to this church, I've logged 2,300 hours attending committee meetings." You'd have thought he was a pilot, instead of a parishioner.

Pause and ponder what an inkling of resourcefulness could have done for that downtrodden soul, that inveterate committee sitter. Without the stickiness of all that planning, he could have viewed the uncut version of "Gone with the Wind" 640 times, or snoozed the equivalent of 288 extra nights, or watched 276,000 thirty-second commercials on the boob tube.

There are at least two schools of thought on every question— the wrong school and *my* school. Friends, I am impressed with the spate of articles and messages declaring, to wit, the minister is being shifted from *minister* to *administer*. All I'm suggesting is that the laymen leave the driving to us preachers, not the mechanical problems.

Strangely enough, I've never pastored a church which had a "committee on committees." Isn't it great to have a super committee to end all committees.

There are situations where the committee on committees appoints the nominating committee, and then the next year the nominating committee plays "turnabout is fair play" and reappoints the committee on committees.

Did you hear about the southern community that bought a snow plow? The area hasn't experienced more than an inch or two of snow in years. But every winter the plow is driven to keep it lubricated. Maybe, dear hearts and gentle people, that's what we should do with administration.

If you're going to mess with administration, go all out! I loathe mediocrity. Your church could pioneer in experimental church administration.

They test racing cars and race horses, don't they? Publicize your trial run at least three days ahead of time. Nearly every television station has conducted drawings from one of those circular wire drums. Either borrow or make your drum. You may construct your drum from a barrel or heavy chicken wire.

Allow the pillars of the church to opt (love that word) pet projects from which a final selection will be made. Narrow the projects down to imperative considerations, for instance:

A. Filling the chuck hole in the parking lot (you know, the chuck hole where the educational director's car was last seen)

B. Retrieving the used bubble gum from beneath the tables in children's department 2

C. Monitoring closed-circuit TV all suspicious activity adjacent to the soft drink machine in the rec building

D. Buying a suit for Adoniram Frak, the chairman of the board and richest man in town

Schedule "Great Experiment Sunday" five days in advance. On that auspicious day Adoniram Frak will spin the drum and choose, at random (of course), the project for promotion.

Guess what program he'll pick? The Adoniram Frak suit special. But, self-effacing man that he is, he'll donate the special to charity. You're right again—the Adoniram Frak Fund, Adoniram Frak, Jr., sole beneficiary!

All jocularity aside, establish goals for which the congregation will strive. Now, just a minute, goals to replace the pastor and staff members are not kosher! Pick one overriding goal which will spark the imagination and interest of the church.

Then, after a lengthy ten-minute deliberation, your Ad Hoc Committee on Ad Hocs will select three experimental teams: (A) the short-range team, (B) the medium-range team, and (C) the long-range team. Each team will receive the same assignment: enlist ten new bowlers for the church's adult bowling team.

Team A is slated to reach its goal before the close of the service. You feel that's impossible? It would astound you how many extraordinary goals are reached in the average service:

Never again will I sit through another one of the pastor's homilies (or is it *hominies*—that is, swollen, worked-over corn?).

I'm going to buy a dress exactly like Prunella Pipgrass', so I can put her out of commission.

We'll eat Sunday dinner at Major Dander's Arizona-Stewed Roadrunner today.

Team B is allowed three to five days, and Team C, ten days to two weeks. Team A will reach its goal, or die trying. Its team members will beg, plead, cajole, and threaten—while the pastor's finishing his sermon.

The longer the planning period, brethren, the more lackadaisical the participants, Team B will probably wait three days before beginning, and Team C will roll into action within twelve days.

In church administration, you'll always operate better under intense pressure. As far as I'm concerned, you folks can plan and project ten years ahead of time, so long as you wait until three days before your target date to actually commence working.

"Let me make it perfectly clear that personnel relationships
are personally interrelated."

—*Hieronymus Basch*

Chapter 5
Pastor-Staph Irrelationships

Isn't it a strange paradox? Young preachers who are "starry-eyed
and vaguely discontented" pine for the day when they will assume
the pastorate of a prestigious "First Church."

They envision themselves with a retinue of staff members to aid
and abet them in the task of ministry (sho' do sound good, don't it?)
. . .

. . . minister of education, minister of music, minister of youth,
minister of recreation, assistant/ associate pastor (according to the
pastor's proclivity), business manager or administrator, private
secretary, semiprivate secretary, financial secretary, dietitian,
kindergarten director, custodial director, janitor A, janitor B,
janitor C, superintendent of grounds, ad infinitum.

Add your own here: _____

_____

_____

Now promenade; sets, round you go!

If and when the strategic "First Church" materializes—with its
burgeoning staff of folks with variegated personalities—the pastor
sometimes wishes he were back at Pilgrim's Rest or Coon Creek or
Lightning churches (especially on Monday mornings).

Ah yes, with no staff members outside of himself and his spouse
(who once served as combination—not on "The Wabash Can-
nonball")—but in the church . . . combination secretary, counselor,
hostess, and dispose-all.

One of my close pastor friends (may he rest in peace) used to
remark, "Listen, there's only one way to survive in this 'stained-

glass' jungle. And that's to stay two steps ahead of your 'board' and staff."

Unfortunately, he was able to stay *only one step ahead!* For me there's one dilemma about that sagacious piece of advice—I never could do the two-step.

Yes, my board and my staff, they comfort me; or do they?

But there are some clerics who have solved the staff situation. When I pastored "way back in the hills," I thought *staff* was spelled *staph*. Leastways, until I looked it up in Webster's (Homan Webster—he had a country store down at the forks). And I came to find out that a *staph* is a germ.

Smart preachers don't have to deal with staff members coming in, as alien influences, from the outside. No ma'am. They keep 'em internal—in the family. Junior serves as supervisor of grounds (really he ain't nothing but the yard boy). Susie is associate custodian (extra talented shaking a feather duster). Pee Wee (he's six feet and eight inches tall . . . plays guard on the basketball team . . . you ought to lay your eyes on the center!) is head custodian.

"Daddy Sang Bass, Mama Sang Tenor" is close to the truth. Only in our case Daddy sings tenor and Mama sings bass (you'll hafta meet Mama, an exceptional woman).

Mama can serve as organist / pianist (and triple in Jew's harp). All of this has magnificent possibilities for large families—like the minister who had nine children. He never lacked a church, because prospective parishes (or charges or churches or pastorates or pastorages) recognized that his acceptance of a call would double the Sunday School enrolment! And talk about a one-family baseball team!

But if you can't con the church into hiring the entire family, and you have to work with a staff, there are certain basic *fiats* to bear in mind. And I'm not speaking about one of those small I-talian cars, either.

Just let the church folks know where you stand in the beginning. You're the boss (in some denominations, a "man of the cloth"). In this case, cloth of *mail* like the Knights of the Round Table wore.

You'll, of course, be responsible for the hiring and firing, job reviews (if such exist), salary raises, and the total supervision of every staff member.

For instance, if you're fortunate enough to have a dietitian, she by all means must answer to you for the consistency of the soup, the crispness of the lettuce in the salad, and the tastiness of the raisin sauce on the ham for the fellowship supper.

Naturally, you'll want to select 95 percent of the music for the music director. But give him a smidgen of latitude—let him pick at least one number a service. And you'll want to sing all the solos you can. You can sing, "I Walked Today Where Jesus Walked," while engineering a free trip to the Holy Land.[1]

Then, too, you can enlist all of your favorite singing groups. And that's regardless of your musical taste, from raga rock Gospel to chamber music by Brahms and Vivaldi. Yes, you'll have a fruitful existence as you personally superintend *everything* (leave no proverbial stone unturned) your staff members do.

Goodie. You can look over your secretary's shoulder when she's typing letters . . . merely to give her moral encouragement. You can publicly admonish your youth and/or recreation director in front of the young people of the church. And you can make your secretary work overtime (without pay, but the deep satisfaction of significant service) to type the manuscript of your latest release, "How to Win Worshipers and Mesmerize Men."[2]

Can't you begin to grasp the fantabulous potential latent in this system? All of these people can serve as sounding boards for your ideas, and as mirrors to reflect your image.

And you will have that possessive relationship. You can think in terms of *my* minister of music, *my* recreation director, *my* sun, *my* moon, *my* stars—oh, excuse me, where was I? It simply gives me goose pimples to consider the majesty and wonder of it all.

Staff meetings? Certainly, you'll conduct regular staff meetings. Have to keep the lines of communication open. Hot line with your fellow-laborers in the joint enterprise. You're part of the team, aren't you?

[1]Cf. chapter on "Rated X."
[2]I typed this one myself.

How will we structure these moments of refreshing interchange, these sessions of free expression, these Matterhorns of sharing which allow the invigorating breezes of inspiration to blow?

Your staff meeting will open with the reading of the minutes by *your* secretary. On second thought, she's a sloppy reader— *you* do it. Then have prayer somewhere in there. There's no one who can put up one like *you* can. Then the reading of Holy Writ. Guess *who?*

Natcherly (sic) you preside, speaking *ex cathedra* for the coming week. You must always remind the staff members who's in the driver's seat (and in your case it ain't Avis or Hertz).

Brother Warble, the minister of music, inquires, "Brother Pastor, why have you changed the youth choir practice to the night of June 31?" Easy. You automatically blame the change on a higher power. Only upon checking your calendar, you discover there is no June 31!

When Mrs. Cal Oree, the dietitian, implores, "Brother Pastor, why did you insist that the church eat chicken cacciatore three straight Wednesday nights?" what's the answer? You reply kindly, but firmly, "You husha you mout'." It's glorious when you have the knack of leading and working with people. Only the chosen few are blessed with this rare gift.

But there is contingent responsibility for assuming this autocratic authority. Since you're in charge of *everything* (there's no personnel committee—rather, you're *it*), you end up getting blamed with *everything.* And I do mean *everything,* beloved brothers.

But it's fun to be in the thick of things, isn't it?

Now if *everything* is going "great guns," it's OK to accept the credit. But whadda you think? It's essential to stay in touch with the troops. Modern communications . . . they're wonderful. Everything revolves around *you* and about *you* and toward *you.* Mostly the last two.

You are bombarded with phone calls, When you said, "Call anytime," you didn't mean 3 o' clock in the morning! Eventually you tear Alexander Graham Bell's picture out of your children's encyclopedia. You are submerged under an avalanche of telegrams, messages scrawled on paper bags, every conceivable missive. And.

as per the trend, various and sundry graffiti (is or are?) plastered about in reference to your pontification.

Sample Questions:

"Reverend, why did you invite that singing group, 'The Righteous Mustard Seed,' to the church last Sunday night? I demand to know. I'm going to withdraw my financial support if that kind of stuff continues!"

Your reply: Simple. Don't fret. "Why, Brother D. Benture, you'll have to call Brother Warble. He's our music director—*totally responsible* for our music program. Yes, Brother Warble is our music director. I'm your pastor. Remember?"

"Brother Pastor, if I have to eat that chicken what's-its-name another time, I'm going to boycott prayer meeting. Might even lead a demonstration in favor of meat loaf. I'm sick to my stomach."

Your reply: Elementary, dear watchman. "Why, sister, just call the dietitian. She's in charge, you know. I don't plan the menu. It's a discount she's receiving on chickens, I'm sure."

"Hey preacher, why was that flower stand donated in memory of my father suddenly painted screaming purple? This is the darkest day in the history of our church!"

Your reply: "You know the answer, brother. See our maintenance supervisor. Yes sir, I believe in placing responsibility where it belongs." Little do they realize that your favorite color is purple.

This type of relationship builds up the *esprit de corps* of your church, all right. It builds *elan vital* in the ranks—from the membership on down to *your* staff members.

Because the staff members are doing so much inept work— what with all the extra supervising you're having to do—you cannot possibly recommend raises for them. You should, however, receive at least a 15 percent increase when budget time rolls around. For what? Why, for having to do ten jobs! And you're hardly being paid for one.

* * *

Epilogue (or is it Epitaph?)

This pastor-staff bit is a snap. And the accrued dividends are limitless. Follow the foregoing approaches and you will . . .

• Have more time for leisure, while recuperating in hospital beds from "nervous exhaustion," "high blood pressure," "heart failure," "mental breakdown" (sometimes called "nervous"), "apoplexy," "ulcers," and the ministerial "heebie jeebies."

• Receive early retirement benefits, because both ends of the candle have finally met and you've *burnt out* before your time (better to "burn out" than "rust out"—clever).

• Better still, pass on early death benefits to your widow and children. Remember how you used to tease with the "little woman" that you were worth more dead than alive. Ha! ha! Ha-a-a-a-a . . .

• Prove a perpetual blessing to your staff members . . .

When you're laid up (in the hospital or grave) they'll be going strong because of your concerted assistance and concern. They'll live to a ripe old age. They'll enjoy their children, grandchildren, and even their great-grandchildren.

They'll play golf, hunt, fish, and loll around the beaches to their hearts' delight. They'll wistfully think of you every now and then . . . when they're at Nassau, Waikiki Beach, or on that world cruise!

"Dr., I wonder if you'd check my incision. Oh, you're the *pastor* of the First Church . . ."

Chapter 6
My Best Bedside Manner
or How I Visit the Hospitals, Clinics, Rest Homes, Veteran's Administration, Baptist, Methodist, Lutheran, Catholic, and Assorted Inpatient and Outpatient Areas!

Preacher, your patient can have a blending of yellow fever, pneumonia, trench mouth, Saint Vitus's dance, and even be sick on top of all that— and bless your strained heart, you're expected to be "Joseph on the spot." And I might add, with your best bedside manner.

My 17,983 hospital visits have ranged from country hospitals with screen doors on the operating rooms to the most massive medical complexes in the nation. You are inquiring, "What's funny about it?" Nothing on the surface.

There's nothing funny about pain, suffering, and death. But it's the *side effects* (not a bad medical term, eh?) that can make you bust your sutures.

You've heard mature adults giggle in the most serious situations, like when a dignified matron drops her dentures during the offertory, or when a preschooler at church hollers out a choice epithet during the sermon, or when two portly dowagers simultaneously sit in the same opera chair in the choir loft.

Really, there's nothing hilarious about a saint being roasted over a fire in the Dark Ages. But one saint-comedian undergoing that grisly death is alleged to have cracked, "Turn me over. I'm done on that side!" A man who could find an element of humor in being burnt alive has my citation as "The World's Most Unusual Christian."

Once a denominational leader confided in me, "Son, if you could visit 36 hours a day, it wouldn't be enough. You'll never catch up, and your members will never let you forget it, either."

Ah, yes, it's memory time. I have in mind one dear matron who established herself as personal judge of my visitation program. Via the party line, her appraisals were all over the church field.

"That preacher is neglecting the elderly and sick. He's not tending to his flock, the old, feeble, and ill."

So, aiming to please, I thoroughly examined my visitation habits. Maybe I wasn't visiting enough. Maybe the shepherd was "dippin' and drappin' the sheep." Perhaps he was failing to care for the crippled lambs and the rams tangled in the thickets.

I redoubled my efforts. I wouldn't miss a soul. You'd have thought I was the ministerial "Dr. Christian." I was there the night before the tonsillectomy, there during the tonsillectomy, and there after the tonsillectomy.

I blew noses, patted hands, stroked brows, and kept night vigils. I was becoming a veritable male counterpart of Florence Nightingale and Clara Barton.

The staff members of the hospitals, clinics, and outpatient areas began to call me by my first name. Several doctors began calling me aside for confidential consultation. What did I think of Brother Blunt's hives? What about Mrs. Wormser's emotional attitude? Who wrote the dirty word on Harry Crimp's cast?

Then, the staff members began inviting me into their lounge (nonalcoholic, I hasten to add). It was reminiscent of the soap operas I'd seen. The medicos were about ready to offer me my own personal smock—green it was. I declined since I would've been out of style, except on March 17.

The nurses inadvertently referred to me as "doctor." I was spending so much time at the hospitals that it was affecting my life-style. There were nights I had to sleep on the living room couch, because, quoth my spouse, "You're beginning to smell like a hospital. You know, I have this thing about hospitals. Remember the day I fainted from the hospital smell at General Hospital? Or was it on Channel 12?"

And I felt incomplete. For the first time I coveted a "little black bag" to complement my Bible. After all, they shouldn't clash. If I'd been an evangelist, with a red Bible, it never would have done. But I was a pastor, and two basic blacks would match.

You can imagine the exhilaration when I heard those little alternating chimes over the speaker system, and then *it* came, "Paging Brother Jay, paging Brother Jay."

As I strode down the lengthy corridor to my appointed rounds, I could almost hear another sound—surging documentary music reverberating in the halls. Oh, shucks, it was the boy with the transistor radio in 301A.

In no time at all, the sister who griped that I was bypassing the sick and afflicted did an about-face. "My, my, that no-count preacher must live at the hospitals, lollygagging and playing nursemaid to the patients! He ought to care for his ministry. He ought to tend to us living folks for a change."

Stop right where you are. In one chapter I'm offering you the ins and outs of the ministry to the sick and suffering. You'll never be the same. You must remember this: Human emotions are tender plants that must be nurtured with TLC (tact, loquacity, and candor).

First, anyone who has flunked nurse's training is not a likely candidate for a hospital ministry. Yes, there are male nurses, too. You have to adjust yourself to the atmosphere of clinic, hospital, sickroom, and outpatient areas.

If you can survive your kid's chemistry set, you're on the road to coping with "that hospital smell."

Second, you ought to have training in acoustics and sound engineering. While on the hospital premises, you should be able to judge your own DB's (decibels), the loudness of your voice. You must learn to whisper loud enough for everyone on the floor to hear you. You know, like the whispers at the public library. I guess you could call it an aside or stage whisper. The folks in the third balcony are supposed to hear you.

Third, you should purchase a pair of those operating room shoes, the kind with the crepe soles. And not because you're going to operate or become a cat burglar, but because of the SF. (That's squeak factor.) I have a preacher friend, a broth of a lad who weighs 392 pounds and sports a size 15 foot. Last month, so it was noised abroad, his shoes alone gave relapses to three patients on the fifth floor of St._____'s Hospital.

Fourth, have valid clearance into the hospitals. There are hospitals where ministers have to register every visit. At one hospital sixteen visits are required before you receive your *very own* clergy pass.

It didn't matter that I had to make an eighty-mile round trip, so I visited patients with ingrown toenails and halitosis. Never shall I forget the day when I was handed my *personal* pass.

With a knot in my throat, with moistness in my eyes, I saluted the ladies at the registration office. With trembling hands, I grasped MY PASS, which would entitle me to visit the hospital without donating blood or being frisked for concealed weapons. I tipped those ladies a whole dollar.

Fifth, make sufficient parking arrangements. So many hospitals have reserved areas for emergency vehicles, delivery trucks, doctors, nurses, technicians, candy stripers, grey ladies, linen vans, and bread trucks. But designated parking spaces for preachers are as scarce as snake hips.

Why not park in the places marked for "Doctors' Vehicles"? You're a "doctor" of souls, aren't you, even though you may not have your degree.

That stratagem beats parking three miles from your patients and hitch-hiking. It was gossiped that one pastor borrowed his druggist's emblem as an entree to parking. That was okay until the authorities threatened to arrest his druggist for filling prescriptions without a license.

Sixth, exercise utmost caution in your dress and personal grooming. Years ago I heard one lecturer advise against wearing clothes similar to those of the undertaker. However, those standards are no longer apropos. Undertakers these days are attired in red shirts, pink slacks, and chartreuse patent leather shoes. Even though the loved ones of a departed Christian should celebrate, I think that's carrying it a bit too far.

Dress stylishly but reasonably. Avoid sweat shirts; blue jeans; red, white, and blue sneakers; and weird Tyrolean hats, except for special occasions. If you wear those items to the hospital, the patients might well mistake you for a doctor.

And avoid pungent-smelling colognes and after-shave lotions. You might give a pronounced setback to an allergy patient.

Beware of unique patterns in clothing. Whatever happened to blue serge and grey flannel and charcoal grey and ministerial black? One of my ministerial brethren wore a sickly-looking green tie with ghastly polka dots. His patient awoke and thought she was having hallucinations.

Follow the admonition of the Boy Scouts and "Be Prepared." Considering the intimate contact of the hospital, you must not be "half safe" or even "three quarters safe." You'll thank me for these hints. And it's advisable to bathe at least twice a month.

Prior to your errands of mercy, if you must comsume sour cream, blue cheese, limburger cheese, garlic bread, and sauerkraut, follow them up by drinking at least a half-pint of that red "soda pop" mouthwash. Yes, drink it.

Prior to his hospital rounds, a minister buddy of mine periodically checks his body's thirteen "danger zones." Sad, he's a natural in Hebrew exegesis, but he can't count past *ten.*

Another ministerial brother operates a veritable rolling toiletries counter in his compact car. He has left nothing to chance in preparing for the saga of the sick.

If it rolls on, glides on, wipes on, or sprays on, it's in his glove compartment. What a provident parson he is.

One glad morning I had the incomparable privilege of riding to a ministerial meeting with my antiseptic pal. En route he sprayed zones three and four (right through his shirt) brushed what teeth he had, and with cream plastered his plate into his mouth, spray-polished his shoes, did conversely with his nose, swigged mouthwash, munched antacid tablets, and ended the ritual by fumigating the car with an aeresol can. And he did all of that while driving. I suspect that the guy showered and dressed in a public telephone booth.

When we reached the hospital, I was a fit candidate for inhalation therapy. Reflect on that old saw, "I can't hear what you're saying, because your smell is so loud." Or something like that.

Seventh, have your person bristling with various and sundry types of reading material. One of my friends was a walking tract rack—tracts in his trousers, pamphlets in his pockets, and an ace—I mean tract—up his sleeve.

He specialized in those drab beauties printed on pulp paper. He wanted to get out the word, didn't he? He scattered tracts with the exuberance of a five-year-old flower girl at a socialite wedding.

The authorities tried to arrest him on a littering charge. My tract friend was thorough; he's even been known to stuff tracts in the nurses' pockets without their being aware of it.

That good brother gave a tract on "You're Becoming a Mother" to a sixteen-year-old girl in the hospital for an appendectomy. It's amazing what his literature did for the patients—outpatients and inpatients. (Up until five years ago I thought the "outpatients" were those who had outhouses reserved in their names.)

"You're Going to Die" and "Meet the Grim Reaper" and "It's Later Than You Think" and "You Ain't Got Long to Stay Here" were the oldies and goodies he distributed to the terminal cases. Yes sir, he believed in striking while the iron was hot.

For laughs you can duplicate your Sunday messages and distribute them to the hernia and appendectomy patients. They'll literally bust their sides laughing.

But, brethren, one of your most monumental ministries lies in the area of a tape ministry. No, stupid, not tape "worm." Record your "sugar stick" sermons and play them, full blast, to the wards of the hospital. If you can't reach them one way, do it another.

That method is guaranteed to produce more repentant patients than the efforts of all the cab drivers in Chicago and New York combined! If your patients have been recalcitrant, your tapes'll scare I don't know what out of them. And, I ask you, didn't they enter the hospital to get cured of what ails them?

Ninth, prepare for every conceivable contingency! Brother, when you're visiting the hospital, you must fend for yourself. Maybe that's why some preachers visit in teams. Doctors operate in teams, don't they?

No doubt you've read that two thirds of the patients have nothing physically wrong with them, that the majority of the patients have imaginary illnesses—neuroses, obsessions, border-line psychoses, and syndromes. And when you complete your rounds, you have a twitch in the right side of your face, you firmly believe the hospital administrator is plotting against you, and you've stopped two of the interns with, "Hey, Doc, I've got this strange pain. It starts here and runs all the way to . . ."

Long have I advocated a hospital visitation "survival kit." My survival kit would contain: (1) sackcloth bedjackets in Joban hues for the women patients who have an immodest tendency[1], (2) a collapsible mop for emergencies, like kicking the bedpan over the bedpost[2], (3) six-ply tissues the size of beach towels[3] and (4) a portable speaker's stand[4].

Now, you latch on to my exhortation. If you'll accept my advice, step by step, you'll have a meaningful ministry to men in misery.

From the split second you drive into the hospital parking lot, you are to project yourself as a pillar of strength. You are the knight in burnished, dented chrome.

Your manner must magnetize the medicos. Away with mundane notions of low-key quietude. When you burst into the waiting room, the staff and visitors must recognize who you are.

The lady at the information desk has seen you only two thousand times, so you have to blare out, "I'm Rev._____, pastor of the _____ Church (loud enough to serve as a testimony for those poor, benighted souls in the waiting room).

"Bless your register, lady, are you well? I thought not. Heh! Heh! (louder) I have the prescription right here (handing her your calling card, a denominational calendar, and five pulp paper tracts). Amen

---

[1] You'd be immodest, too, if you'd given birth to five children, had twelve different operations, and been examined by every intern, extern, and outtern, including orderlies, in the hospital.

[2] In most hospital leagues, a three-point play

[3] Not for the patient, but for you while eating the patient's leftovers, and crying over soap operas and football games on the rented TV

[4] After all you preach far better from a rostrum. Your seventeen-point sickroom sermons are far easier to launch from a solid pad.

and Amen!'" You've been in the hospital only 74 seconds, and already you've charmed the people.

Then, with all of the aplomb of Bronco Nagurski at a seated tea, you bound forth to dispel gloom and disseminate the effulgence of your reflected glory.

You could have gone golfing or fishing or hunting, but you are on a mission of mercy. You have mastered my nine "ins" and "outs" of hospital visitation. You, my spiritual sawbones, are an omnibus of comfort and consolation. And besides, your golf clubs, shot gun, and rod and reel are in the trunk of the car.

Underline these ne'er-to-be-forgotten pointers. Even if you visit on seventeen floors, the staff must be acutely aware of your presence.

Consider these greetings to the nurses:

"Ah, there's our little angel of mercy."[5]

"Is every thing coming out all right?"[6]

"I'm let down. Pick me up and give me a high."[7]

Now stop at this juncture and let your mind roll on. Create other clever witticisms that will ingratiate you with the nurses.

Consider your salutations to the orderlies.

(To an orderly carrying a bedpan down the hall): "Hey man, look out for that extension cord!"

(To another): "Ugghh, do you still serve those barium milk shakes? At least you could've added cherry flavor."

(To another): "Great, baby, you handle that bedpan like Kareem Jabbar handles a basketball!"

See there, by the moment you reach the first room you've made a splash (and if you rate, a literal one)! One professor suggested that the visitor always tap lightly on the door. Make sure the patient is ready for visitors and is not as leep.

Naw! If they'd have wanted privacy, they'd have put locks on the doors to hospital rooms. Walk on in. The nurses don't knock, do they? After all, if you knock, it might scare the wits out of the

---

[5]She weighs in at 285 without her white shoes.
[6]To the nurses rolling a gall bladder patient from surgery.
[7]To the nurse carrying the medication tray.

patients.

You're compassionate, but also cosmopolitan. And by using the "high test gasoline" approach (no knock) you will elicit the most spirited responses from your patients. For instance:

"My goodness, Brother Jay, it's you. My, my . . ."

"No, I'm thrilled beyond words that you're here, pastor, Would you set this pan over there? Thanks."

"Embarrassed? Why certainly not. I'm naturally red like this."

"Pastor, I know you think this unusual. Yes, I'm aware that this' the only Bible you've ever seen with a centerfold like that . . . ."

"Brother Jay, help me wipe this lipstick off of my face. Oh, you haven't met my first cousin the nurse? Brother Jay, meet my first cousin the nurse. Er—hon, what'd you say your name was?"

"Think nothing of it, pastor. This is the usual treatment after surgery."

Are you beginning to see? The chill is already thawed and rapport is established. Mark this passage in red.

There are special greetings to the patients that no articulate minister should be without.

"Shucks, old girl, you're looking mighty pale. But exposure to heat'll change all that, eh?"

"Gee whiz, don't you look like a pipeline with all of those hoses and tubes sticking out of you?"

"Cheer up, old buddy, rigor mortis won't set in for three or four days yet."

(To the plastic surgery patient): "Say, Mrs. Snort, you've got the cutest nose on the side of your face."

"Ha! Ha! Two more years in this place and you'll have the whole annex paid for."

"Mercy, Herman, you look like a walking quilting party."

"Nonsense, there's nothing wrong with you that a good dose of religion wouldn't cure."

"Herkimer, I believe in telling it like it is. Pardner, you ain't been tithing."

"Yeah, that Dr. Filch is something, isn't he? Mrs. Blomp, heh, heh, I guess the Doc took everything you had but your false teeth."

If you're creative in dealing with human suffering, the supply of salutations is legion.

Let's become pragmatic about it. You got 'em where you want 'em, at least for the time being. You have to make them suspect that they're on their deathbeds.

Then, if they repent, it'll be all the more dramatic, and also provide a better sermon illustration. Which sounds better? "Horace repented while recovering from chicken pox" or "Horace, with the death rattle in his throat and the dew of death on his brow, repented and was miraculously snatched from the burning." Brother, I don't have to answer that question.

You shouldn't wear out your welcome, of course. Your hospital calls—per patient—shouldn't last more than forty-five minutes each. Exceptions are if the patient is watching the World Series or eating dinner. Then, a prolonged session may be indicated.

One of my preacher brethren used to check with the hospital dietitian ahead of time. That preacher's visitation intensified on fried-chicken and roast-beef days.

To each his own, but one of my brethren of the cloth nearly always sits on the edge of the patient's bed. His patients are downright overjoyed with his folksy, down-to-earth approach. And hand-holding and brow-stroking are prominent in his repertoire.

Mushrooming hospital costs are a boon, because either for lack of money or lack of room, patients are thrown together, and all the merrier for you to have a congregation. Your therapeutic ministry is magnified ten and twelvefold.

"What a big mouth you have, preacher."

"All the better to preach with, my dear!"

Yes, brother, while you are scattering precious seed, why not broadcast them over the ward and into the surrounding annexes? You are proclaiming, with *magna voce,* "I have arrived. There's no need to fear. You folks have waited all your lives for this golden moment."

And it's beautiful to gather the relatives and play "Can You Top This?" Conduct your contest in the middle of the ward, because you want your effervescence to be contagious. See who can come up with the most hilarious joke, and also give awards for the most raucous laughter. This game is likewise suggested for all-night wakes at the funeral parlor.

After your salutation, your sermon, and your sanctified silliness, then follows your supplication. One young preacher mastered this art.

We were visiting a man who was in the hospital for a routine check-up. In a tone of finality, the youngster prayed, "Lord, bless Brother _____. And please, Lord, don't let him die. Amen." The suddenly pale-faced patient almost did—die, that is.

I'll remember this incident until Dr. Scholl's stamps out corns from the face of the earth. I was visiting a grandmotherly saint in a county-seat hospital. By actual count, there were twenty-three of her relatives in the room with her.

All of them ignored the patient. Gossip, jokes, and the grapevine filled the air not all ready occupied by their cigarette and cigar smoke. I managed to cough out a brief benediction for the patient.

And I heard the patient gasp as I strode out of sight, "Mercy, I'll be so glad when I can get out of here, and go home to get well!"

"I zee mine role, not in offering solutions to counselee's problems, but in serving as a zounding board."

—*Dr. Reinhold Fraud*

Chapter 7

Now Here's the Answer: A B C

"Hello, Joe, this is Al, got a problem." Those were the inimitable words of a character during the heyday of radio "sitcoms."

Al didn't waste those words, either. Problems, problems, problems. They make the human race a rat race.

Frail, human words, flimsy conveyances they are, could never express the munificent influence that you preachers have on your parishioners, and on others. Yes, you will always *be in demand*.

Let me rephrase that. People will always be *after* you, for various reasons, of course.

Because of your salary, the bill collectors will be after you. When you visit, anticlerical canines (with four legs) will be *after* you. And (*sigh*) some of the world's most irascible critters will be *after you!*

The phone in your humble manse jangles at 3 o'clock in the A. M. Your clogged ears are greeted with, "Oh, pastor, I hope you weren't asleep. I've just got to talk with someone." No, certainly you weren't asleep. You're a night person. Pastors stay up all night long, and sleep all day.

"How charming of you to call, Mrs. Flak," you intone, adjusting your ministerial mien.

"Yes, it has been unseasonably warm. Uh huh. Uhhh huhhh. Yes ma'am. Yes ma'am. Absolutely. Right, I understand. You're indubitably correct. Surely."

"Who? Oh, I'm dreadfully sorry. You want me to pray for Homer's health. Yes ma'am. I can assure you that I'll put him on the top of my prayer list. You can rely on me, dear lady."

When Mrs. Flak finishes, it's nigh on to 4 A. M. You turn to face your helpmeet. Isn't she adorable lying there with those spears coming out of her hair and slime all over her face. She reminds you of Phyllis Diller's stand-in.

"Hon, that was Mrs. Flak (no reply). Sweetie, Mrs. Flak telephoned (not a snort). Baby, Sister Flak wants us to pray for Homer (n. c.). Doll face (nary a grunt), who is Homer? Oh, forget it, stupid!"

Preacher, that's how the crumpet crunches. People are beset with problems, and you had better have the answers, or else. Even though you're ashamed to admit it, you don't have the fuzziest idea who Homer is, but you'll pray for him. You might run by to visit him, if you knew his whereabouts. Blessings on you, Homer, whoever you are and wherever you are. And, good morning, Homer. Flop!

No two people in the world are exactly alike, and glory hallelujah! Therefore, you must prepare for the monumental ministry of having four billion compact answers.

They took a survey in one area where I persecuted the saints. The question was, "How many pastors are trained in counseling and pastoral psychology?" I was the only one with training.

What qualified me? I was confined to quarters with the "American" flu (I had passed it on to two residents of Hong Kong). The only channel our TV received had soap operas from 10 A. M. to 4 P. M. In ten days I had become versed in marital infidelity, pregnancy, abortion, suicide, depression, bankruptcy, juvenile delinquency, and narcotics addiction.

No wonder housewives are the best counselors!

My training in the seminary was extensive. You know, seminary's the place where your questions are answered with, "Why are you asking that? If you didn't get that in college, it's too late, now."

In college you asked the same questions, and heard this immortal reply, "Be patient. They'll answer that in the seminary." So, my college and seminary training prepared me to become an artful dodger and a sleight-of-hand expert.

It stands to reason that your counselees (that means the folks that you counsel) have to become impressed with your psychological and psychiatric credentials. You must advertise in your sermons, in the bulletin, and vis-a-vis.

Set up your counseling hours. Apprise your church members of your availability. You *want* to help. In fact, if they don't let you help, you'll scream and stomp.

During your counseling sessions, you'll have to dispense with playing solitaire with your prospect cards. You'll have to hide your radio with the ear plug, and abandon those old *National Geographic* magazines. This will demand Spartan discipline on your part.

Your counselees must see in you a way-out blending of Jung, Adler, Freud, Bill Sunday, and Phillips Brooks.

From the pulpit make copious references to your recent counseling situations. Naturally, you wouldn't be so indelicate as to mention names, but you simply must build up your counseling ministry.

Little innuendos like these will suffice:

"Ah yes, only last week one of our young members came to my study. Bless his heart, he plays right tackle on the high school football team (you thought I was going to say "right guard," didn't you?). He and a certain young lady— well— are in bad trouble. But, through my encouragement and understanding, those *three* young lives will be salvaged."

"She appeared three days ago. Tears coursed down her cheeks as she sobbed out her confession. Minutes before she had climbed from her pink Jaguar and sauntered toward the church. Tsskk, tsskk, the luridness of her confession made me wince. But now it's different. She has traded her pink Jaguar for a purple MG."

"April 15th has come and gone, and so has our money. Heh! Heh! But there's one beloved brother in our town who still has his—money, that is. Two weeks ago, in the strictest confidence, he blurted out the entire story.   He owns a department store in town. (NOTE: There's not but one in that town.) This man of prominence admitted to cheating the government for the last ten years. I'm sure he's sorry, but, "Be sure your sins will find you out."[1]

---

[1]At this point a visitor leaves his pew and moves to the rear of the sanctuary. He is an agent with the Internal Revenue Service, and *was* passing through.

"Yes, brothers and sisters, you can confide in me. Reveal to me the deep, dark secrets and I'll never tell. My confidence is a sacred trust. So, I'll be in the study to receive you from the hours of . . ." Mind you, those where only representative gems of your pulpit publicity.

Everything must be in readiness for your counselees. Situated prominently on the front of your desk must be such volumes as: "Simple Solutions to Slippery Situations," "Is This Suicide Really Necessary?" "I Traded My Phobias for Photography" (now I have a phobia about double exposures), "Easy-to-Understand Psychological Aberrations," and "You Think You Got Problems?" by Claim Whynott—along with them, a copy of Holy Writ.

It's unfortunate many Protestant churches have prohibitions against beards for ministers. A beard automatically looks psychiatric, or New Testament, or just plain itchy. And when you sport a beard, you can sit behind it and smirk and snicker, and they'll never know the difference.

You've seen those stilted pictures where a guy is posed resting his chin on his hand, with his first finger extended over his cheekbone. That photo screams out, "Here is a sage, a savant, a man of cosmopolitan learning and transcendental insight." Here, also, is a man who feels stupid and who has a doggone tired hand!

As a counselor you will never arrive until you master the technique of emphasizing one-or two-word responses, complete with all of the nuances and inflections. There's the raised eyebrow (right or left, depending upon the mood), the twisted mouth corner, the elongated crow's foot, and the corrugated forehead.

"Yesssss." "I see." "Hmmm." "Go on." "Certainly." Noooo?"

You may expand these to include:

"Tell me about it." That's like hollering "sic 'em" to a Doberman pincer, or—the masterpiece of them all, "Oh, you do feel that . . .?"

For your edification I offer the following counseling session. PAT. is for "patient," because anybody that sees you has got to be patient. PAS. is for "pastor."

PAT.: Pastor, I don't know what I'm going to do!

PAS.: Yesssss.

PAT.: I-I'm at the end of my rope, at my breaking point!

PAS.: I see.

PAT.: The world's caving in on me. All hope is gone. Despair descends around me.

PAS.: Hmmmm.

PAT.: I can't eat, I can't sleep. Specters lurk in the shadows. The hounds camp on the doorstep of my tortured conscience.

PAS.: Certainly.

PAT.: My soul, preacher, can't you hear me! I implore you!

PAS.: Yessss.

PAT.: Preacher, I—I feel as though I'm losing my mind . . . that I'm going to die.

PAS.: Oh, you do feel that you're going to die, do you?

PAT.: Yes, yes, I do. It's awful.

PAS.: Tell me about it.

PAT.: Oh, pastor, I can't bear to tell you. It's—it's—

PAS.: Noooo?

PAT.: I'm baring my heart to you.

PAS.: Go on.

PAT.: But, pastor, I don't want to go on!

PAS.: Oh, you do feel that you don't want to go on, do you?

PAT.: Now, I'm becoming confused.

PAS.: Oh, you do feel that you're becoming confused?

PAT.: Yesssss.

PAS.: Noooo?

PAT.: Are you contradicting me?

PAS.: Tell me about it.

PAT.: Galloping grizzlies, I am trying, but you won't let me!

PAS.: Certainly.

PAT.: Well, I wanna tell you something. I came to you for help. And all you do is sit over there. You know what? You sound like a parakeet.

PAS.: Oh, you do feel that I sound like a parakeet, do you?

PAT.: Yesssss.

PAS.: Hey, would you mind if I told you about these bad dreams I've been having?

PAT.: Impossible. You're impossible! Whatever was bothering me is not bothering me anymore. I'm going to leave here and walk in the sun once more. Chin up. Head held high. You're the sick one. Sick, sick, sick . . . . .

PAS. (*to himself*): Isn't it wonderful what this non-directive method of counseling will do? Hmmm, think I'll make a phone call.

PAS. *(now talking on phone): Goot morgen, Herr Doktor.* How's tricks? When's my next session with you? No, Doctor Froelich, I've quit carrying my teddy bear to bed with me. Now I'm sleeping with my stuffed tiger. Yes, Doctor, we'll talk about it Thursday at 2 o'clock. *Danka schoen!*

In order that you might polish your counseling technique, let us recap that amazingly successful session. After all, isn't it true that the counselor is to serve as a "sounding board"? All most counselees want to do, anyhow, is talk it out. Avoid giving them "pat" answers.

As one noted counselor observed, "Never, never let the counselee know what you're thinking about. Make him worry about what you're thinking about. Yes, you must refine the art of listening. Notice how well the pastor of the preceding session listened, using the finely-honed inflections and nuances.

His counselee or patient was able to release his steam. Isn't that what he wanted to do in the first place? Did you recognize, too, the variety of responses the pastor gave. Clever, wasn't it, how he kept feeding back the counselee's emotions?

And the pastor used only 62 words during the session. He was a perfect "board," giving off with the "wooden" responses. He didn't allow the patient to lean on him. After all, the counselor is to solve no problems. The patient's supposed to do that.

How dazzlingly brilliant of the pastor to help the patient explode—release his problem. The pastor was willing to sacrifice himself in order that the patient might be made whole. Remember what the patient yelled out, "Whatever was bothering me is not bothering me anymore. You're the sick one. Sick, sick, sick . . . ."

There the patient's problem was gone. Where did it go? Surely you've figured it out. It was transferred *to the pastor,* who immediately resorted to calling *his* counselor.

Here's another counseling jewel. A young couple is ushered into the pastor's inner sanctum. Remember, no two cases are alike. This pastor employs the directive approach. He is sold on the value of verbal "shock treatment."

PASTOR: Come in, come in. I've been meditating and praying for this opportunity. Yes, "a couple a day keeps the doctor away." What's bothering you, young people?

HUSBAND: Why, nothing much, really.

PASTOR: Oh, now, you can open up and share it with me. My heart is empathetic. My arms are outstretched to the two of you. Yes, my intuition tells me that there's sin in your young lives.

WIFE: But, pastor, that's not it at all!

HUSBAND: That's right, pastor. We're doing well.

PASTOR: My, my, don't try to hide. Yes, that's the human tendency. You might as well spill all of it. It'll be a catharsis for the both of you.

WIFE: A what? Goodness, whatever it is, it sounds bad.

PASTOR: Come now, it's wicked enough for you two to lack an adjustment in your marriage. But to be self-righteous along with it is—is too much!

HUSBAND: But, pastor, please.

PASTOR: Listen, no amount of arguing is going to stop me from saving your marriage. Do you realize that two out of three marriages are on the rocks?

WIFE: Is the percentage that serious?

PASTOR: You'd better believe it. Young man, what about those nights that you're away from home?

HUSBAND: What is this? I'm away from home only when absolutely necessary, like when I'm on the road for the company or have to work late.

PASTOR: Uh huh. C'mon. All you young bucks are alike. 'Fess up. What've you been up to?

HUSBAND: Hey, slow down there, preacher.

WIFE: Charlie, what have you been up to?

HUSBAND: Nothing, Debbie, nothing but my work.

PASTOR: Chuckle, I've never heard running around called work before. But what about you, young woman, while your husband is gone? I read only the other day that 39 percent of all young wives—er—carry on.

HUSBAND: Yeah, Debbie. Now the shoe goes on the other foot. Whatta you been doing while I'm away? And what about those two nights I tried to call home and nobody was there?

PASTOR: Yes, my dear, the truth will out.

WIFE: The truth. Why, the truth is I was gone to the drive-in store and—and—to visit Hazel Pidley.

PASTOR: Uhhh huhhh.

HUSBAND: I'm really wondering now. Debbie, I think we'd better get to the bottom of this. And all the time I thought I could trust you!

WIFE: What about me, Charlie, you low-down Casanova. Working late, my foot!

PASTOR: Now, my children, isn't it heart-warming to throw open the windows of truth. That's why I'm here. Marital counseling, as you've already guessed, is my specialty.

HUSBAND: Preacher, I want to thank you for exposing Debbie for what she is. From now on I'm going to call her Jezebel.

PASTOR: Think nothing of it, my son.

WIFE: Pastor, until this shocking revelation, I—I thought Charlie and I had a happy home. We came by just to discuss plans for the young adult Sunday School party. But, thanks to you, I'm going to contact a lawyer the first thing Monday morning.

HUSBAND: That's a capital idea.

(*Debbie and Charlie are rather verbal with each other as they exit the educational plant.*)

PASTOR (to himself): Yes, I'm a discerner of the thoughts and intents of the human heart. Chalk up another victory for virtue. There's nothing like the refreshing breezes of honesty. It's just as well. If it hadn't been for my counsel, those precious youngsters might have continued in the slough of deceit.

The foregoing cases serve as superlative examples of directive and nondirective counseling. Take your pick according to the extenuating circumstances.

And don't you dare refer your counselees to those "professional" counselors. You are the original "Dr. I. Q." You are a veritable tower of strength. Repeat to yourself, "If I don't have the answer, nobody does. If I don't have the answer . . ."

Why, these preachers that are always making referrals simply demonstrate that they're not infallible. They're not able to cope with the human psyche.

Through my method of "meaningul manipulation," however, you can master the minds of men in a moment. Slurp! That would make a dandy sermon title.

Memorize this chapter verbatim. Meditate on the suggested approaches to counseling. Muse over the two case studies. And you will become the "compleat (sic) counselor."

Make your sessions uncluttered as possible. Instead of employing those ink blot tests, manufacture your own ink blots. Pour ink on your patients' clothing, and while it dries, introduce yourself.

By the time the ink dries on the contra—clothing—you're ready for the patient to work the perception puzzle. You know, the puzzle where the squares go into squares, the circles go into circles, etc. Only in your crummy puzzle, the circles go into the squares, and the squares go into the rectangles, and the triangles go into the trapezoids.

And your counseling program is not complete without a series of those fold-out charts. Only in this case the charts are illustrated with diseases instead of dispensations. The emotional and mental diseases are listed alphabetically: A is for amnesia, C is for catatonia, and D is for depression.

For home visits (you can carry mental health to them) a set of condensed flip charts is available. Your patients will literally _flip_ over them. Your charts are laden with simplistic answers to complex problems. Your technique is as "snappy" as Alpha, Beta, Gamma, Delta, and far easier to interpret.

Phellow physicians of the psyche (Phellow is like Phideaux in

South Louisiana), these Aleph, Beth, Gimel methods of therapy work like a charm. To demonstrate how easy these methods are, I hereby chronicle the therapeutic ministry of an ex-friend.

Once this former compatriot was rather happy-go-lucky, but he read in a counseling journal, "The astute counselor must empathize with his counselee. As it were, he must suffer, bleed, and die with his counselee."

My ex-crony became a past master of the counseling skill. And then he encountered a case that would've boggled Freud's cranium. His case was a modern-day Lady Macbeth.

Every knowledgeable psychologist pines for a case like hers. Name a phobia, and she had it. And hate—brother! Come to think of it, she hated her sisters, too. She hated people she'd never heard of.

The lady declared that she kept hearing "little voices." I do, too, only I have three growing boys. In concert the leaders of Red China, Russia, and the United States were conniving against her.

She refused to drink from a water fountain. And she was probably sane at that point, since most of our water is polluted. To cap it all, she believed herself to be Tinker Belle.

Do you think our staunch brother referred that pitiful creature? Nope. With the background of one counseling course in Bible college, and armed with the rich lore of this chapter, our mind-mending Moses escorted his Lady Macbeth out of the wilderness.

How dare we even suggest a referral? Besides she couldn't afford $35.00 to $50.00 an hour, only a T-bone steak every now and then.

Our friend put himself in that lady's shoes, but he sure looked funny wearing size 6 AAAA high-heel pumps on the streets. And it like to crippled him for life, to boot.

By religiously adhering to the meaningful method of manipulation, plus unswerving reliance upon the ABC charts, ink-blot tests, and perception puzzles, my ex-friend cured his patient. My ex-friend is ex because he hates me. The fact is, now he hates everybody!

It all came to a head when I had occasion to counsel with that brother. Here follows a "bugged" portion of our session.

ME: How're you doing?

BROTHER: Whatta you mean by that?

ME: Nothing. I merely wondered how you're feeling.

BRO: Feeling? Why, am I supposed to be sick?

ME: Well, no, not to my knowledge.

BRO: I never felt better in any of my other *eight* lives. Only . . .

ME: Only what?

BRO: Why are you so suspicious? Only . . . that there's an insidious
  international conspiracy being perpetrated.

ME: What conspiracy?

BRO: You ought to know, the one against me, and you're in on it.

ME: You're kidding.

BRO: No, I'm not. Can't you hear those voices, those little voices?

ME: I'm afraid not, brother.

BRO: You're crazy, I hear them in eight-track stereo. And Russia,
  Red China, the United States, and *you* are out to nail me.

ME: Oh, nooo!

There's the case of a counselor who handled his patient too well.

*   *   *

I doubt it, but do you recall the pastor of this chapter's opening
paragraphs? Mrs. Flak called at 3 A.M. to request prayers for
Homer. You don't remember? That's about how well my members
recall my sermons from introduction to conclusion.

Ten nights later the phone jangles at the more respectable hour of
2 A. M. Mrs. Flak sobs out the grim purpose of her call. "Pastor,
Homer's dead. Boo hoo! You must hurry over right away."

Great gobs of goosegrease, you mutter to yourself. *I intended to
visit Homer, but put it off. Mrs. Flak will never forgive me for my
sinful neglect and procrastination.*

By the time you reach Mrs. Flak's abode, your passenger car has
racing "slicks." With shoes untied and one pajama leg jutting below
your trouser cuff, you hobble into Mrs. Flak's home.

"Oh, I'm dreadfully sorry about Homer, Mrs. Flak. At a time
like this, I wouldn't be anywhere else. Bless your sweet heart." Mrs.
Flak liquidly blows her nose.

Your heart is playing pitty-pat as Mrs. Flak ushers you back to view (*shudder*) Homer's still-warm corpse. The pangs of guilt wrack your conscience. How could you be so calloused and insensitive as to have neglected Homer?

There is Homer, glassy-eyed. You have to prop yourself against the cupboard. The Homer that you have prayed for, but neglected to visit, is a dead goldfish!

MEMBER: "Hello, I must speak with the pastor."
ANSWERING SERVICE: "I'm sorry. The *person* you are calling is not in service at this time. Do not worry. Read Romans 8:28. This is a recording."

Chapter 8

Pastor, I Know You're Busy, but . . .

"The Hurrier I Go, the Behinder I Get" was the motto near the grease rack of a garage. Where else had I seen that watchword. Why, in a pastor's office!

The pastor's work is akin to that of the housewife. It's never done. There's a backwoods expression, "I'm so busy I meet myself coming and going in the road." That's certainly not hard for me considering my size.

The pastor who boasts that his work is "caught up" is a fibber, unless he has laid to rest all of his parishioners and prospects. And then he'd have to labor full-time keeping himself straight.

You've heard, "If you want it to rain, wash your car." By the same token, "If you want to be re-called, go on vacation or to a convention." If you make the mistake of leaving phone numbers or an itinerary behind, either "Ma Bell" or the state police will track you down. That's why the mainstream ministers are traveling incognito.

Assuredly, ministers must stay on the defensive "36" hours a day. Why 36 hours? Because the pastor is expected to cram a day and a half into one. Ho! Ho! You've heard the unfunny jest: "There are three kinds of people—men, women, and preachers." And sometimes you actually begin to believe it!

But trends are changing. If a pastor has a staff, his fellowworkers must protect him from the intrusions of members. In many churches, the church secretary is *bodyguard* to the minister. In less hectic days, the average church secretary was a pretty little thing. The pastor and personnel committee inquired about her office and typing skills. Could she use shorthand? Gregg or Pittman? How fast was she (at shorthand, of course)? Rate of speed in typing?

But no more. The committee queries, "In what sports did you participate? How many pounds can you press? Judo? Karate? Kung fu?" If only our country would lift the immigration barriers. Today, I believe the members of the USSR Women's Weightlifting Team would come closest to qualifying as pastors' secretaries. That is, if we could convert them from their atheism.

Nowadays the church or pastoral secretary is rated more on her ability to "cover" for the pastor, rather than absurd nonessentials like typing and shorthand. The pastor's time is sacred, and the average secretary is the "angel" with the flaming sword. She is to drape a protective canopy over the pastor's schedule.

The church may have less than 100 resident members, representing 33 different families, but the pastor must excel as administrator. The pastor is the only individual I know of that *personally* is responsible for a *corporate* image. Regardless of his "charge," he must give appearance of being the busiest man in the community.

Because our obese country is on a "health" kick, the minister should jog or sprint everywhere, even when he's behind the wheel of his compact car. And he cannot slow down for the rustle of a Bible page. If the minister is to be preeminently the administrator, he must emit a cool professionalism.

"Pastor, I'm distressed. I simply *have* to talk with you."

"I'm sorry, Mrs. Schmidlap, check with Miss Gooch, my secretary. She must handle my commitments. Good day."

"I'm sorry, Mrs. Schmidlap. The pastor is booked solid. But he can give you fifteen minutes on September 28."

"September 28, but that's six months away. Why, my dentist can see me sooner than that! I have a severe spiritual problem. I must counsel with the pastor!"

"I'm sorry, I'm sure that your dentist can help you. Why not confide in him?" (Click.)

One pastor's waiting room reminded me of a depression bread line. An emaciated woman remarked, "Brother _____'s such a busy man of God. I've had this

appointment two months. Another three hours' wait won't hurt."
Yes, Brother _____ at that moment was exceedingly busy wedging out of a sand trap on the back nine at Putrid Acres Country Club.

Because of the demands on your time, the President of the United States would have to make an appointment through your secretary to see you. But you'd travel to Washington and expect the commander-in-chief to immediately receive you into the Blue Room.

A committee from a prospective parish dropped in on Brother _____ at his office. They happened to glance at his desk calendar and were touched with Brother _____'s piosity. For every day was scrawled in long hand the word, "God." What total commitment! Brother _____ would qualify as a doctor writing prescriptions. What he had written was "Golf."

(See my chapter on "That Image Is Fuzzy.") Since your work, preacher, is never done, why try? You must leave time for your family. What about Sunday and Wednesday nights (because those are normally church nights, anyhow)?

I had a preacher frater whose philosophy was beautiful. He believed that the *whole world* was his "family," most particularly his "brothers" who golfed, hunted, and fished. Think of his missionary outreach as he fished, hunted, and golfed at least six days a week.

Meetings are imperative, especially committee meetings where we restructure the universe. Another activist minister of my acquaintance was gone to meeting nearly every night—the Strange Fellows, the Jaguar's Club, the National Association for the Advancement of Country Preachers, the Sanskrit Isegetical Society, to name a few. His wife decided to start attending meetings. The first one was with her mother, and the second, with her lawyer.

How, then, can you, O harried pastor, arrange a sensible schedule? Every night while you're watching one of those palaver shows, write on separate slips of paper the activities for the following day. The following morning post them on a dart board.

The slips you hit select as activities for the day. If you fail to land on golfing, hunting, or fishing, try bowling for a change.

Congregational expectations vary, according to the location of the church. In the open country, the preacher is smart if he hunts or fishes with the key people of the church. I've often wondered why outdoor ability wasn't included in his call.

To put it in the words of Brother Zeb, "Preacher, you ain't the worst preacher I ever heard, but you're the awf'lest fisherman I've laid my eyes on." In many rural communities, remember that golf is still suspect, because it has the connotation of the city.

In town there is a blending of ministries—hunting, fishing, bowling, and golf sometimes thrown in for respectability. Even if your church is in the "sticks," it's in vogue to call it a "suburban" church.

It has oft' been said, "If your golf game is lousy, you must be keeping up with your ministry. If your game is too good, it proves that you're neglecting your church." My golf game (until I gave it up for Lent) was invariably lousy, and I also doubt if I was keeping up with my ministry.

Beware of those you beat on the links. Let the chairman of the "board" win. And that goes for the Bishop, too, if your church happens to have episcopal government. Let the chairman or the Bishop have the "gimme's." The preachers with the lowest golf scores are liable to remain in the lowest levels of the hierarchy!

In order to "fabricate" a schedule, it is advisable to make out a *tabula rosa* for the day. Have nothing on the calendar, and then work from there, because you'll never make it, anyway.

And you can borrow office practices from certain small-town doctors. Don't make appointments, but have the people drop in and wait for you. Under this system, it's not a bad idea having a soft drink machine and a sandwich franchise in the adjoining office. Let the people become rooted while they're waiting for a transplant into the tree of life.

After spending the entire day, they'll appreciate you all the more. Plan on giving them the stock medical greeting, "My good lady, now what seems to be your trouble?" To which they can answer characteristically, "Doc, I don't know what's the trouble. If I knew, I wouldn't be coming to you."

If you're cagey, you can wind up each case in five to seven minutes. And you can label every hidden problem as a virus. As the people leave, admonish them, "Now go home, get lots of rest, drink plenty of liquids, and take aspirin." No sweat.

In one of my more activistic pastorates, I was often called upon to counsel with people all hours of the day, and into the small hours of the morning. After one all-night session, I had just settled down for a short winter's nap, when suddenly there came a tap-tap-tapping at my chamber door. 'Twasn't the "Raven," though I had wished it 'twere.

In my concentration camp P. J.'s I hobbled to the portal. In the darkness stood one of our church leaders. "That's really something. You preachers sleep all day long. We have to work for a living." How could I argue with him? He had hit the sack by 8 o'clock the night before.

The preacher who performed our wedding ceremony (he sent my check back in the mail—would accept nothing) related how he fixed a critic's cart. His critic was always mouthing the old routine: "You preachers don't do anything but sleep late, take coffee breaks, hunt, and fish, Wish I could get by with that. *I have to work for a living.*" Don't you just love to mull over that last line?

So my preacher friend invited his critic to spend a typical preacher's day with him. They started a 7 in the A. M. and wound up about 10 P. M. The formerly captious layman, with tongue hanging out, panted, "I'll never say anything about you preachers again. I've learned my lesson!"

What that layman didn't know won't hurt him. My preacher friend wanted to bolster his case, so naturally he stacked the day, and probably packed *three* work days into one.

Yes sirree, stay supercharged, dynamic, bustling, always in a hurry. Imitate the dear brother with whom I had the privilege of ministering. He went everywhere in a sprint. If you walked down the street, he'd run off and leave you in the lurch.

Even though the pace of city life is frenetic, the country and small town situations pose a different set of problems. In the city the pastor is not seen as much by the membership-at-large. In the small situation, the pastor and his family are still watched with close scrutiny.

When you arise, when you lie down at night, when your car departs and returns, when you empty the garbage, when you yell at the children . . .

Oh, well . . . One of my preacher buddies had it all together. His church expected the preacher to start out early in the morning, because most of the members were plantation owners or small businessmen.

Said preacher would get up with the sun, park his car by the church building, and then walk home and grab four more hours of shuteye. The people were too busy to check on his whereabouts. Besides, they didn't want to disturb his "meditation and prayer" in the study.

Oh, forgive me. Gotta go now. I'm in such a rush, in demand all the time. . . .

"Reverend, your five o'clock shadow and beetle brow make you look sinister. All the powders of Rubenstein will not sweeten that little face of yours!"

—Helma Prude, Make-up Artist

Chapter 9

The Image Is Fuzzy, or,
"Imago Pastoris"

"Public relations." That phrase first fell upon my innocent ears when I was a teen-age theologue. For shame, I thought that public relations was what people ought to keep private. I've come a long way, baby.

Now our glossary of terms has to include "image," whether individual or corporate, public relations, and *ad libido*. But when I launched my ministerial barque, church PR programs were in their infancy.

You put an occasional article in the county paper, or the daily paper, if you lived in a town that large. Ten thousand or more population—to me that's gigantic! You publicized dinners-on-the-ground, box suppers, homecomings, and the revival meetings, usually in connection with the homecomings. And people were too interested in coming home and reuniting to concentrate on revival.

Freshly aware of PR, I once requested $15.00 from the "board"; I wanted to publicize the summer revival in our church. The request was tabled, and in that church when anything was *tabled,* it was buried. In that church, in fact, funerals were designated as "tablings."

Since I was doubling as church secretary, too, they suggested I cut a stencil and mimeograph leaflets. Nasty notes left by "night riders" on horseback had higher quality than my splotched leaflets. To boot, I sacrificed two Sunday shirts on that mimeo's altar, and all for the sake of public relations.

Yes, Jesus did declare that we ought to learn from the children of this world. But sometimes I wonder if we're not learning too well. Yep, we ought to be wise as snakes and harmless as doves. But a few of us are becoming awfully snakish doves.

Brother, you must have an image that comes across slick and professional. I mean, you have to become the embodiment of an 8 by 10 glossy. In my case, 8 by 10 is measured by the foot.

Remember, your constituents are watching you. Never, never give an impression that you have a flaw. You should learn from the example of certain on-the-ball clerics. They have an entourage of image-builders—advance men, front men, follow-up men, and even side men.

Oh, you can't swing that? Never fear. Who is the best person to publicize you? Who is sold on you the most? No, not your mother, love her, but YOU.

Haven't you guessed who writes most of the copy about ministerial achievements? Come now. Note this all-inclusive article which appeared in a denominational journal.

"Advances during Dr. Zilch's ministry have been phenomenal. Attendance at all organizations and services has skyrocketed. The baptismal waters have churned constantly. During Dr. Zilch's ministry, the massive educational annex was completed, the sizable church debt was paid off, and extensive new equipment was purchased.

"Multitudes of people responded to Brother Zilch's ministry. New musical instruments were purchased. The existing church plant was renovated within and without. A complete youth ministry was inaugurated.

"Three mission points were established. Major records were smashed during his ministry. Now, because of great demands upon Brother Zilch, he is sharing his ministry with untold thousands of churches and denominational groups.

"He is leaving First Church to form the Dr. Abner Zilch Evangelical Foundation, dedicated to the purpose of furthering Zilch's dynamic ministry."

You don't need twenty questions to guess who authored that. His last name starts with "Z."

Strip away the PR accoutrements, and here is how the account should read.

"Advances during Dr. Zilch's ministry have been rare. Attendance increased by 100 the week after Dr. Zilch resigned. The baptismal waters churned constantly, because the church was having trouble with the plumbing. The educational annex consists of one room, the church didn't have a debt to begin with, and the new equipment was a paint brush, five hymn books with shaped notes and an oil cloth table covering.

"Multitudes of people responded to Brother Zilch's ministry by quitting the church or moving their membership. The musical instruments were a twenty-nine cent horn and a whistle left over from Hallowe'en, both ticketed for the nursery. The existing church plant was redecorated *within* budget (zero dollars) and *without* anything being done. The complete youth ministry consisted of Dr. Zilch's seven children, who periodically gathered in the church kitchen for banana sandwiches and root beer.

"The mission points were at the City Cafe, where Brother Zilch religiously drank his coffee; the Kitoma Club, where he was a member; and the Bogey Acres Golf Club, where Brother Zilch shot buzzards. (Not literal buzzards, but my terminology for three over par on one hole. You say, 'Great, isn't the world his parish?' Agreed, but I question if those three locations would qualify as bona fide mission points. Maybe so, since preachers today are even holding forth in discotheques, bars, taverns, saloons, and strip joints.)

"Major records smashed during his ministry were when the church audiovisual director, carrying a stack of 33 1/3 rpm albums, tumbled down a flight of stairs. Now, because of great demands for Brother Zilch to vacate his pulpit, he is *having* to leave.

"He is leaving First Church to form the Dr. Abner Zilch Evangelical Foundation, and it's truly' dedicated to furthering his ministry. Nobody else will further it but Zilch himself. But it's comforting to realize that he will have the support of his mother, his wife, and *five* of his children."

Every four years a historian writes about the "making of the president." What about the making of a preacher? You must become known in order to wield the mace of influence. Keep them cards and letters goin' in.

If nothing else, discover the newspapers that print "Letters to the Editor." Follow the suit of one preacher in a deep south state. By Gutenberg, that preacher must multilith his epistles and transmit them to every newspaper this side of eternity.

He's appearing in print on subjects like ips bark beetles, the Coriolis effect, and occasionally, religion. Editors are always interested in fillers. And that same preacher sneaks in the peculiar doctrines of his church.

The apostle Paul admonished us to become all things to all men. This world is crazy, anyway. So, the only means of touching people is to be crazy along with them. You can do this in so many intriguing ways. Curiousity killed the cat, so kill them cats!

I'm not a Dogmatist. I never could become interested in that particular sect. But I wish to share my tried and true P R approaches. You can call immediate attention to your church and (*chuckle*) yourself with newspaper ads like these:

"Come to First Church Sunday Night. Our Electrifying Pastor, Brother_____, Will Turn You on with This Pulsating Preachment: 'Watts Your Short Circuit?' " or

"You will literally thrill to Brother _____'s sermon topic: 'Sin, Zen, and When'," or

(*Complete with gigantic picture of yourself*) "Who Is This Man? Aren't You the Least Bit Curious? The Revelation Is Scheduled for Sunday at First Church."

The supply is limitless. It's according to whether you want to project a folksy or sophisticated image. Now, if you want to impress the public with your sophistication, you've got to use the word "relevant," in everything you do.

Yes sir, bind it as frontlets between your eyes. And stick with it. I checked its synonyms in the dictionary. They were "germane, pertinent, apposite, applicable, apropos." Yuk, I decided to stay with relevant.

My soul lept for sheer joy when I heard one theologue employ that word fifteen times . . . in his introduction alone!

If you covet folksiness, something that will keep you in touch is demonstrations. If the city officials will give you a permit, splendid. But if they won't, go to it, anyhow.

Here's an exclusive list of special attention-getters, and you, beloved brethren and sistern, are privy to it. Remember now, you're carrying on these demonstrations for the "cause."

If people call you a fool, that's okay. Didn't they call Galileo a fool? Didn't they call Copernicus a fool? Didn't they call Edison a fool? Didn't they call Percival Finkbinder a fool? Who's Percival Finkbinder? I haven't the foggiest—I just wanted to make sure you're with me.

1. Form a motorcycle caravan and clog traffic on the main street during rush hour. Wear Nazi helmets (without the swastika, most assuredly) and black leather jackets with "Heaven's Angels" on the back. Optional jacket logos are: "Bible Bikers," "Hallelujah Hondas," "Christian Cyclers," and "Whosoever Will Wagons."

2. Let your Sunday School organization conduct an attendance campaign with a neighboring church's Sunday School. Call the event "Don't Let Us Get Your Goat." You guessed it. The losing church "gets the goat," smell, tin cans, and all, during the morning worship service—and, I might add, keeps that prize in the ladies' missionary society parlor for an entire week.

3. Cash in on nostalgia. Since memories are in vogue, you can come up with techniques going back to the dawn of history, although I wouldn't suggest Adam and Eve prior to the fig leaves.

If you want to tug at heartstrings, hark back to Captin Marvel, who is now extinct. Before changing into Captain Marvel, crippled little Billy Batson would shout, "Shazam!"

Our aforementioned Dr. Zilch built an entire ad campaign around that watchword. For instance, "*See How Amazing Zilch Magnetizes Men*." He used that motto upon fielding on-the-spot questions on TV.

Zilch was truly amazing as he answered questions concerning Red China, Ghana, Togo, Lower Slobbovia, birth control, the common market, the population explosion, and the development of the laser beam. But the program went off the air when a preadolescent inquired, "Dr. Zilch, can you tell me where the Book of Hezekiah is found?" and Dr. Zilch proceeded to tell him.

Or, there was the preacher who had trouble with his "official board," which numbered one less than two dozen. He dipped back into the twenties for his slogan: "Twenty-three Skidoo." Oh you kid, get it?

4. If you really want to make an impact, collaborate with your church's teen-agers. They are adventurous and enterprising and bent on fun things. They're a far cry from when you were a teenager, lolling around nurturing your acne bumps.

Here's an extravaganza for openers. Have your teen-agers fan out into the shopping centers. There, with youthful zest, they can slap "good news" stickers on all of the cars, trucks, grocery carts, and baby carriages.

Shouldn't they request permission of the drivers? Naw. Would you rob those people of a surprise? And reflect on all of the good will you'll engender, when those surprised shoppers view those bumper stickers proclaiming:

"Watch my smoke. I'm on fire for First Church," or

"Wash me . . . I want to be clean when I attend First Church," or

"Honk four times for the Gospels . . . courtesy of First Church."

5. Of a less spectacular nature is your participation in community affairs. Just think of the preacher who led in prayer at the dedication of a brewery. Three weeks later, in another state, he preached on the evils of beverage alcohol.

You cannot, must not miss an opportunity to be seen. You must adapt yourself as a social animal. The guests with the highest rank are expected to be barely on time— or better still, late.

At every function make your grand entrance. Everyone will be overwhelmed with your air of . . . especially if you forgot to apply the roll-on.

If you've gone to bless a cup of pink lemonade, it must appear in the society pages—all the better if you're in the center flanked by those divine dowagers. And bully if you're wearing the proper clerical vestments.

If you've caught a fish . . . the sports page.

If you've caught a cold . . . the hospital admissions column.

If you've crossed Jordan's stormy banks . . . bold-face type in the obituary column.

Yes, your adoring public is dying to gaze at your benign ministerial visage. Incidentally, one fellow preacher pointed out that the clerics of a certain denomination were trained to remain in the limelight.

Amen. Yes sir, those preachers could upstage the parting of the Red Sea and the thunder from Mount Sinai. Around them in public you stand about as much of a chance as a drunk mouse around fifty extremely sober, and hungry, tomcats.

You, brother, must be seen everywhere and in everything. You must be ubiquitous—all things to all men, omnipresent, and omniscient.

As a matter of fact, though, this image-building will call for a restructuring of priorities. My late dad always advised me, "Son, if you don't build yourself up, nobody else will."

Full-time image building will mean less of things like prayer, Bible study, meditation, comforting the sick, and reaching the stray sheep. But you'll merely have to make up your head about the necessity of belonging to five civic clubs, a hunting and fishing lodge, golf club, public affairs forum, and holding honorary membership in sixteen organizations, all of which require your presence for a two-and-a-half-minute prayer.

And another thought. Why worry about humility? Because if you project humility, your constituents are going to call it "false modesty." Isn't it refreshing to be honest?

Everything you say and do rates the superlatives. Remember, if you ascend into heaven, be careful of your "press." If you descend into the deep, the religion reporter must be there. Brother, everything is fabulous, gigantic, titanic, marvelous, magnificent, wonderful, and colossal!

I sat, bug-eyed, before the television, Maybe I was jealous. I was watching the end result of Madison Avenue suavity, which came across like Bleecker Street crudity. The audience was at a high peak of expectancy, and there was even a fanfare and applause.

The religious ringmaster intoned, "Ladies and gentlemen, here is the man of the hour, the man of the day, the man of the week, the man of the month, the man of the year, the man of the decade, and the man of the century—Brother _____!" Funny to me, he didn't even seem to be the man of the second.

And since your people hang on every single, solitary word that oozes from your lips, give them a double portion. Every week, since hearing you was woefully insufficient, have your messages printed and circulated to every member.

I heard about the precious brother who'd been at his church only three months, and began his summer reruns. He asked his members to list their favorite messages. Shucks, most of us can't remember what we preach from Sumday to Sunday, much less expect our members to recall their favorites.

The favorites with my people have been those sermons that ended in time for the beginning of pro football and pork chops.

I've always marvelled at those preachers in churches which observe pastor appreciation day every year. Again, maybe I'm green-eyed. Some of my congregations have appreciated me so much more when I've moved to other churches. Strange how they love and respect me now.

Presently I have one appreciated brother in mind. I believe he's the most appreciated and respected preacher I've ever seen. His churches always remember the exact day his anniversary rolls around. Mine have always remembered, too, but for different reasons. That appreciated preacher's picture appears on the front of his church mail-out paper, and inside there is a glowing article concerning his achievements.

You implore, "What's wrong with that?" Nothing, except in his case that's every week! Well, it's nice work if you can get it.

And it's great to make a production out of invitations to speak for revival meetings, conventions, and retreats. Every preacher worth his salt must have personalized brochures and pamphlets, along with glossy prints and mats. You have to be prepared for moveable type or offset printing.

And you expect your P R profiles to be utilized for maximum exposure. It's absolutely imperative for the members down at

Rocky Knob to know:

. . . that you are listed in "Who's Who in the Everglades," that you belong to six Greek organizations (one of which is Anastasia's delicatessen); that you are widely in demand for revival meetings, retreats, clinics, conferences, reunions, dinners-on-the-ground, various and sundry church socials, civic clubs, and taffy pullings; that your thesis in the seminary was entitled, "The Dialectical Spiritualism Latent Within the Symbolism of Siegfried Garbosch's Theory of Superfundamodalism"; and that you have done considerable study at Hertingen, Loblollich, and Spumoni Universities (and you have all the scars to prove it!).

You see, that profile will project you as an other-worldly, pedantic peripatetic. The folks at Rocky Knob'll expect condensed lectures of your seminary thesis.

The good part about it is: you'll delight the blazes out of them if you can preach a lick. But if you can't preach, they still won't be disappointed.

"My gilt-edged clergy sticker has opened up vast new vistas."
—*A Satisfied Saint*

Chapter 10

Rated X

or Things Preachers Always Wanted to Know, but Were Afraid to Ask

"Enter in, all ye who have hope."

In the chasms of your consicience, answer one query, "Am I mature?" Neither would it hurt of inquire, "Am I over-ripe? Am I rotten?"

Ten years ago they would have circulated this chapter "under the table" at conventions, general assemblies, conferences, associations, synods, and presbyteries, according to the denomination.

This chapter would've been banned in Boston, criticized in Cripple Creek, opposed in Opelousas, sneered at in Schenectady, jeered in Jefferson City, and taunted in Tallahassee.

But we are overjoyed to report that, after years of suppression, the content of this chapter is now available to adventuresome clergy and laity. If you are immature, offend easily, or have a squemish stomach, call ' halt at the end of this sentence. But if you wish to become privy to esoteric wisdom, proceed.

But wait! First, you must promise to use this information advisedly. In the wrong hands, what you are about to read would prove disastrous. Second, will you promise to protect the innocent and unsuspecting from this inflammatory material?

Naivete was our middle name when Mary Sue and I moved to our first pastorate. Matrimonial veterans of five months, we had no time to think about money. The parsonage, back in the hills of Tallahatchie County,[1] was without a refrigerator, so we decided to open a charge account.

---

[1]Not far from where Billy Joe allegedly jumped off that bridge. . . since there were probably 1000 B. J.'s in that county, we have no idea which B. J. jumped.

When the 'frig arrived, we noticed an extra charge on the ticket. Surely the store had erred. I was about to call the store until I remembered that we didn't have a phone. In fact, nobody in the community did, except the railroad agent.

After driving hurriedly into town, I burst into the store. "What's this?" I implored, pointing to the extra charge on the ticket.

"Why, that's the carrying charges," replied the clerk.

To which I replied, "Whatta you mean *carrying charges?* Some of the church people carried it for us in their pickup truck!"

As a boy of the cloth, I had been baptized into the waters of high finance. Within months I had become a wheeler-dealer. In my avaricious hands were two $100 bills, the first I ever laid my eyes on.

I had sold a black Pontiac sedan to the proprietor of a pool hall, and had received the same loot I had paid for the wreck a year before. At least the car's radio played beautifully.

In a minister's manual, I noticed a squib on "How the Pastor Handles His Money." It's mighty hard to handle something you seldom have.

It was at a Protestant pastors' conference that the brethren heard about a Jewish rabbi whose salary—not counting his benefits—was $65,00 a year. You wouldn't believe what that did for the cause of Zionism.

Three of those preachers, so I understand, changed their names to Cohen, Feldman, and Bimstein respectively. In the seminary most of them despised the study of Hebrew.[2] In that conference there was a revival of Hebraic studies. "Shalom" became the stock greeting, and for their pastoral suppers they started serving motzah ball soup, lox and bagels, blintzes, and knishes.

"Amens" and "hallelujahs," unfortunately, will not settle your accounts. The average ministerial family makes far less than the median income in the United States.

For ministerial families in lower-income brackets, this is a swell game. When the phone rings, the preacher answers the phone. If

---

[2]You know, that's the language in which a "fly speck" can change the course of human civilization.

he's not there, his wife does. The rest of the family members try to guess which bill collector is on the phone. The PK (preacher's kid) who guesses the most bill collectors during the week receives a special prize. He is allowed to play with the cancelled charga-plates for three whole days!

How vividly I recall the halcyon days of yore. In one church my salary was $45.00 a week. The finance committee met secretly and voted to cut it. One pious matron who favored the economy move publicly declared, "We'll keep the preacher supplied with eggs." I don't even remember whether she had any chickens.

Hopefully, maybe we won't have to hear this prayer anymore. "Lord, you keep the preacher humble, and we'll keep him poor. Amen." All too often, O brother, you are expected to keep up with the Joneses (filet mignon) on a baloney budget.

Amidst skyrocketing prizes, however, it is a comfort to realize that your budget would supply you with the "extremities." Like chicken necks, pig snouts, pig ears, pig tails, pig feet, neck bones, and north ends of chickens flying south.

The casual reader may contend, "But most preachers are overweight, if not downright obese." You would be, too, from a steady diet of the extremities and rice and potatoes and bread and spaghetti and macaroni and . . . the cheapest staples available.

Some denominations have a salary minimum for the ministers. The congregation is supposed to pay at least X dollars per year. I've served a few places where they, too, have a minimum. I believe I've heard it called, "the rock bottom minimum."

In my earlier days, the congreation nearly always wanted a "full-time" pastor . . . on a "quarter-time" salary. It was considered taboo for the pastor or his helpmeet to work on the side. I've heard tell of pastor's wives taking in washing, and pastors who sneaked off at night and on Saturday to peddle encyclopedias, cook ware, and ladies' shoes.

Really, every man who is serious about his calling should be impressed into selling ladies' shoes. PMS (Pre Mini Skirt) I sold ladies' shoes at two department stores on Canal Street in New Orleans . . . to keep body and soul together during seminary.

A cleric who can do that without jumping into the Mississippi River is bound to succeed in the ministry. To no avail I suggested to my professors that selling ladies' shoes be included as a requirement in the course of field mission work.

What, then, can the minister do to feather his rather porous nest?

1. **Marry a rich woman.** Muhammad married an older woman. She financed his meditation and preaching, and hubby was able to found an entire religion. As a youthful theologue, I married Mary Sue for her beauty, charm, brains, and sweetness—but her car didn't hurt.

In college we divinity students (I always liked caramel or chocolate better) filled out "Ministerial Student" cards. Alas, when the card inquired, "Do you own a car?" I had to check no. While my colleagues were driving to their preaching points, I hitch-hiked, walked, and used public transportation like the bus, train and mule.

And my vehicular brethren were being "called" to churches while still in college. No church would have me unless I could *drive* up into the church yard. I had considered riding a bike, but wouldn't I have looked ridiculous riding a girl's bike?

You may have married a girl of poverty, but hang onto her, especially if she has a strong back. The Lord is your invisible means of support, and your wife, the visible!

2. **Dabble in business ventures—bonds, mutual funds, franchises, and stocks.**

It always impresses me to overhear my ministerial brethren referring to their business ventures.

"Yes sir, I invested in 50 shares of blue chip stock—Amalgamated Flub, Inc."[3]

"Brother, the little woman and I have put our money into a terrific company. Listen, there's no obligation. Could we come by and talk with you. It could be the answer to all your money problems."[4]

"Hey, I want you and the Mrs. to drop by the pastorium. We've converted Joey's room into a nursery. Ha! We're expecting, but

[3]Worth ten cents a share!
[4]Funny, but it's the first time that brother has ever given you the time of day.

Ethel's not pregnant. It's our chinchilla, "Charo." Where's Joey sleeping? Oh, he's such an adaptable little rascal— under the carport, in the trunk of the car . . ."[5]

With wild anticipation my ministerial friend spied the ad:

"Part-time work. Minimum effort and investment involved for guaranteed maximum return. Service vending machines a few hours a week. Make full-time salary for part-time work."

His minimum investment, $1,000, was begged from the bank. Shortly and to his chagrin, he was receiving part-time pay for full-time labor. He was back where he started from. In addition he was accused of operating games of chance, since the odds of obtaining candy from his machines were ten to one.

In yesteryear it delighted me when Rev. and Mrs. Register (an alias) called our humble parsonage. They were passing through, and wanted the wife and me to join them at that high-falutin' restaurant on the interstate. Brother Register insisted on treating us. In his own words, "Brother, I've never done anything for you. And I want this to be on me."

As we drove to the restaurant, I commented, "That's really something, sweetie. A man of Dr. Register's importance wanting to set us up for lunch. Do you suppose he's going to recommend me to a strategic church, or maybe for a denominational position? You know, hon, I've always felt that Dr. Register's had high hopes for me." We tingled with excitement.

Dr. and Mrs. Register greeted us as though we were long-lost loved ones. And about midway through the petit pois and ribs au jus, Dr. Register's eyes twinkled. The news for which we had waited was about to explode in our ears.

"Yes, Dr., what is it?"

"Brother Jay, you're one of the most outstanding young ministers in our denomination. I have the utmost confidence in your ability. My, you have performed a memorable service here at your church, which I feel is one of the pivotal churches in this area."

---

[5]That poor brother found out that Charo was a pygmy rabbit, and Joey liked living outside better than in.

"Why, I'm flattered, Dr. You shouldn't say that— I'm just an humble servant." (He should've said it, because I had done a "Whale" of a job. And the only humility I had was of the mock variety.)

"Since you mean so much to me," brightened Dr. Register, "I want to share this with you and your radiantly beautiful wife . . ."

"Yes sir, it would please me." (Slurp, slurp, on which committee or board would I serve. To what key church had he recommended me? Was he hoping to dub me as his successor in the higher echelons? Three seconds' waiting was transformed into an eternity.)

"Brother Jay, this is a memorable occasion. I—my wife and I have found the answer to all of our money problems, and we'd like to. . . ." My wife made a hornet-line for the nearest powder room, and the ruddiness of my face drained into my feet.

After expressing our reluctance to invest, we noted that Dr. and Mrs. Register quickly dismissed themselves— "pressing business, you know, ole buddy."

As icicles formed in my coffee, and as I counted the leftover *petit pois*—one by one—I spied them . . . the tickets for the meal.

3. **Seek a salary for your wife.**

"Preacher, we like you, but we love your wife." "Behind every successful pastor is a woman—pushing."[6] "Preacher, there's this vacancy, and we're sure that your wife'll be tickled to . . ." "Reverend, I don't know how we could stand you without your wife. She's a heap prettier than you. Har! Har!"

I used to keep a file on those comments but quit years ago. The little woman is the power behind the pulpit. My wife has given me far more sermon ideas than Charles Spurgeon or Clovis Chappell or C. E. McCartney.

More than one pulpit committee has queried, "Can your wife play the piano?" Considering my preaching, her piano playing would have to be the determining factor in my call.

There are parishes which automatically expect the ministerial matron to be prexy of the missionary society, coordinator of the

---

[6] If he's single, it's his mother.

nursery, teacher and leader morning and night, and counselor to the membership in case of her husband's absence.

During the flu season, when many young mothers confine their children to quarters, the pastor's wife is expected to be there with her children, complete with their nonstop noses and diarrhea. Yes, the pastor's wife must crusade like Joan of Arc, conduct her household like Susannah Wesley, and dedicate her children as Hannah did Samuel in the Old Testament.

From the outset, churches affirm, "We're calling you, preacher. We'll accept your wife." Who's kiddin' who? Although the church "officially" extends a call to the preacher, isn't it really a package deal? You better believe it.

They may call me "Porky," but I guarantee that I'm not a "male chauvinist."[7] The minister's wife is the only unpaid fulltime staff member. At this point I'm with women's lib, Ms and all.

If a stipend for the pastor's wife were figured into the church budget, it could help ease the ministerial financial burden. Let me hear all you Ms's give with an "Awomen."

4. **Organize a clergymen's union.**

Now there's an organized union for every occupation, including doing nothing. I burnt my bubble gum cards when the major league players struck for higher pension benefits. That was a blow to the fan who had memorized every batting average, along with his Scripture verse cards, in the history of baseball.

Secretaries of sanitarial science,[8] teachers, policemen, hod carriers, and hoods have gone on strike. Although demonstrative, ministers have never organized to strike against their churches. I fear, though, that a large number may have struck against the Highest Management of all.

A few enterprising ecclesiastics have sporadically struck. A certain dissatisfied dominie would periodically resign his charge. In business session, the church would call him back and raise his salary. This worked no less than six times. Seven turned out to be

---

[7] I don't have my chauvinist's license yet.

[8] Commonly known as garbage collectors.

his unlucky number.

Another pioneer vacated his pulpit, thumbtacking his list of grievances to the vestibule bulletin board. *A la Luther!* The usual labor demands were catalogued: salary increase, more desirable office conditions, a longer vacation, and multiplied fringe benefits. The preacher refused to fill the pulpit, but did not resign the church. No pay, no preach.

That preacher was the only one-man picket line in the history of organized labor. During services he carried two and three placards at a time, and sometimes a "sandwich board." His picket signs were not extraordinarily creative. They read: "Central Church Unfair to Unorganized Labor," "Pay the Preacher or Perish," "Put Your Money Where My Mouth Is, " and "Benefits Are Blessings."

About 50 percent of his "bench members" either stayed at home (because they didn't want to get involved) or refused to step across the picket line—not because they were sympathetic to the striking preacher, but because they had to *force* themselves to attend, anyway. And since they attended out of habit, they were able to "kick it" during the strike.

A religion reporter happened to interview the chairman of that church's "board."

REPORTER: Mr. Staid, what effect has the pastor's strike had on your church? Surely, it's tragic not hearing the word.

STAID: On the contrary, it's probably the greatest occurrence in the long history of our church. That first service without preaching was strange. We had a responsive reading, a Gloria Patri or two, the recitation of the church covenant, and a hymn or two.

REP.: But didn't you miss the proclamation from the pulpit?

STAID: Not really. And pretty soon we were down to one Gloria Patri, one hymn, and an abbreviation of the church covenant.

REP: But didn't you consider having other ministers fill the vacuum?

STAID: With the pastor *in* the pulpit there *was* a vacuum. Without him there was a vacuum. The difference was: the vacuum didn't take forty-five minutes. Yes, at first we thought about calling in other ministers, but . . .

REP.: But why didn't you?

STAID: For a time we felt our preacher was—well—the next thing to nothing. But when he went on strike, and then we had nothing, we realized that he was *worse than nothing*. We decided to stick with nothing.

REP.: Excuse me for editorializing, but it appears that your church is going backward.

STAID: Thats not always bad. It's according to the game you're playing. We're backward and proud of it. In our area, even the birds fly backwards. At least you can see where you've been!

REP.: But what about the spiritual life of your church?

STAID: Quit rocking the boat. You ultra-liberals scream about liberation, and now our church is liberated. We're doing without preaching, and not even missing it. At least we're honest—we always wanted as little religion as possible.

REP.: What will you do about your pastor's demands?

STAID: We may not become excited and rave like you foreigners, but we're good people. We're not going to meet his demands. In our last "board" meeting, we agreed—well . . .

REP.: Yes, agreed to what?

STAID: Well, you remember that comedian that was paid $100,000-a-year if he'd agree to stay off of TV? We agreed to pay our striking pastor his present salary and benefits *not* to preach!

REP.: Huh?

On second thought, brethren, maybe we'd best remain the only unorganized professionals in America.

5. **Cultivate the gratuities.**

My late dad was a pragmatic Christian. He advised, "Son, if your members want to give you something, take it. If you don't, it'll hurt their feelings." During my ministry I've hurt no feelings by rejecting gifts.

I've ended up with my share of uplucked chickens and ducks, fish complete with insides and outsides, rigid rabbits, stiff squirrels, and every conceivable gratuity but an unmounted moose head. Honest, we were thankful. And I was never polite enough to turn down watermelon(s), lima beans, corn, tomatoes, squash, etc. Or beef, or veal, or mutton, or pheasant, or partridge, or buffalo.

Following my day's admonition, I not only took what they gave me, but I learned the art of dropping hints. And you have to be the right man in the right place at the right time.

Corn and watermelon are luxuriant, and you "just happen to drop by" a farmer-member's homestead. You leisurely stroll into the pasture with your rancher-member and rapturously gush, "Yum, those are the most succulent looking Hereford's in the world. Bet those steaks make the best eating anywhere." Or, it's a cold day and you're visiting, so you loudly sniff and ask, "Hmmm, is that coffee I smell?" You wouldn't be so forward as the brother who hits the front door and hollers, "You got any coffee in the house?"

Hint, hint, hint. Choice advertising does not beat you over the head. It lures you with tantalizing suggestions. Preacher, if you are to survive, you must master subliminal psychology. You must lead your people to think *they're* doing these things for you, when, really, you're planting these benign thoughts.

Until recently it was rare for a preacher to make a pilgrimage to "The Holy Land." For years I figured that "The Holy Land" was Nashville, where the Grand Ole Opry is located.

In religious periodicals you see these advertisements for a trip to The Holy Land, conducted by Brother _____, your amiable host and tour guide. In most cases Brother _____ couldn't correctly guide you to his church's rest room facilities. And yet, for $964, he's going to conduct you throughout Europe, the Middle East, and Coney Island.

The catch is: Brother_____ is the "front man" for a tour agency. If the Brother enlists fifty traveling companions, his trip is free. But I'm lazy, and not photogenic, either. So, I'll use ESP to lay the groundwork for my trip.

I'll have a series of Holy Land bulletin covers for the worship services. I'll preach on the following themes, "The Holy Land in Prophecy," "Will the Bronx Become a Suburb of Israel?" "The Holy Land Beckons Me," and "Nothing Could Be Finer Than to Be in Caesarea in the Morning."

I'll induce the organist to play "I Walked Today Where Jesus Walked" for six straight Sundays. Either I or the minister of music will sing the same song every other week, and we'll mouth the words on the six Sundays the organist obliges.

I'll enlist speakers on Bible Lands archaeology, complete with artifacts,[9] water from the Sea of Galilee and the Jordan River[10] and dried wild flowers plucked from the Mount of Olives.[11]

Bless your mustard seed, I can almost feel my feet touch Olivet. I can feel my toes wiggling in the waters of the Jordan, and I can feel an Arab bullet whistle by my ear.

But guess what'll probably happen? It's the story of my life. After my campaign of Holy Land saturation, the church leaders will call me into a confidential meeting. I can hear the chairman now:

"Brother Jay, your emphasis on the Holy Land has sold us. (I grin from hair to hair—that's right, only have two). We are enchanted and enthralled by the land where our Lord lived and ministered. And it's all because of your faithful ministry of inspiration and teaching. Next summer (here it comes) . . . the 'board' members and our wives are making a trip to the Holy Land. Brother Jay, because of your indispensable ministry here, we believe that you would rather remain with the—choke—people who need you. We're giving you a raise of $5.00 a month, and—sigh—here's a little reminder."

"It's more than I can stand," you blubber. Later, you open "the little reminder," and discover that it's a one way ticket to Pismo Beach.

Take all they give you, brother.

Avail yourself of the ministerial discount. After all, you're in a special category. It's necessary to establish your identity, by all means, since you're a man of low means. Clergy automobile tags are spiffy, because they're virtually indestructible. But clergy decals, clergy bumper stickers, clergy buttons, and clergy pins will suffice.

Too bad they haven't come up with clergy armbands and clergy

[9]A "true piece of the cross," actually driftwood from Louisiana.
[10]From Lake Erie and the local sewage lagoon, respectively.
[11]Blossoms from winds at the local dump.

cummerbunds for auspicious occasions. Your blatant advertising will indubitably elevate you in the eyes of the populace. Once you're established as a "clergyman," you're ready to negotiate for the discounts.

In a public business I beheld a clergyman loudly demanding his "rights." He stormed out, with a mob watching, because the clerk would not honor his ministerial credentials. After that shocking display, I tore off my clergy bumper sticker.

Thank the Lord for honest businessmen. Years ago I asked a proprietor if he were quoting me the "church price" on a piece of equipment. He replied, "There's only one price, the church price and the regular price. I figure that nobody but churches and preachers are going to buy this machine, anyway." A smart old rascal, wasn't he?

The Bible does teach, "Ask and ye shall receive." For over half of my ministry, I was reticent about asking. Besides, when you make demands upon a church, the worst it can do is answer no . . . or run you out of the country.

About every year we wend our way back to Tallahatchie County and visit the first community I ever served as pastor. About one fourth of my former members are now in the "arms of Jesus." The three fourths who remain will not mind my sharing this experience with you (that is, if you're still with me).

Necessity is the *grandmother* of invention. At our first parsonage, the bathroom facilities were outside behind the house, although I do not remember if the door had a half-moon. When availing ourselves of said facilities, the structure would shift, and the ground beneath would crumble. It reminded you of the parable concerning the sinking sand!

Without my having to petition the church, the members moved into action. At a night business session, a gracious lady stood and spoke of dire necessity. This is her appeal almost verbatim.

"I move that we build a bathroom onto the parsonage, because that outhouse is becoming dangerous, and we don't want to lose our dear pastor and his wife!"

To this day, I don't know what she meant by that last phrase!

Adenoids

Sic gloria transom Tuesdi.

—*Anonymous Latin Poet*

Why "Adenoids"? Because I never believed in being a "copy cat." I've perused barrels of books whose authors should be sued for plagiarism. Why, about every other book ends with an "Appendix." How uncreative—and dishonest.

The word "adenoids" is defined as "an abnormally large growth." You're probably patting your foot and hollering that this growth should have been cut off after the "Preamble." If it never occurred to you that this "growth" is satire, I'm going to apply for an unlisted phone number. And I'm going to wear dark glasses and an Edward G. Robinson hat pulled down low over my eyes.

In case you're wondering, I do love the Lord Jesus Christ. I love the ministry of reconcilation. I love the church for whom Christ died. And I also love to laugh. The only people who have a valid reason to laugh are Christians.

You are probably grateful that nowhere in this book did I quote from Rabbie Burns' "To a Louse upon Seeing One on a Woman's Bonnet in Church." That's done to death by preachers and teachers. But it still has a universal application.

Loyal readers, even in the ludicrous and ridiculous, there can still be a kernel of truth. If only all of us could see ourselves as others see us, to paraphrase Burns.

And I can never forget the colorful illustration of a mountain preacher. "Why are you folks fidgety? Isn't it funny when you fire a shotgun into a pack of dogs, the ones that get hit, holler." Preacher. Layman. Yours truly. If we "protest too much" it could imply that we're hit.

You might call *Preacher, You're the Best Pasture We've Ever Had* a volume on "How *Not* to Do It in the Ministry." On "how not to" I am eminently qualified. At least, I'm willing to admit it. And I'm willing to implicate myself along with my imperfect brethren, "who put their legs in their breeches one leg at a time."

Brethren, all of us want to leave our "footprints in the sands of time." The majority of us have left ours in the mud. Thank God, at least we're no longer in the quagmire. I myself have made an impact, and I'll illustrate.

In a small-town pastorate, I did my share to assist the custodian and "board." It was on a spring afternoon when the ladies of the church were preparing the "fellowship hall" for a bridal shower that night. And we experienced more than a bridal shower. The rain kept falling on our roof.

Like a ministerial Boy Scout, I climbed into the attic to check for the drip-drip-drip we were hearing. I was walking on 2 by 6's but forgot there were no cross pieces. Precisely as I found the leak, I fell through the ceiling.

Because of my corpulence, I failed to finish the trip. There I was "in suspension" hanging from the ceiling. I couldn't get up and I couldn't get down. And nails were piercing me in the stomach, as my legs flailed in mid-air.

About that time a gracious lady stepped into the side door. A retired school teacher, she had a high tolerance, but what she beheld was more than she could stand. She moaned to herself, as she later testified, "Why, oh why did the preacher have to come to church to commit suicide? Now, where can I find a knife to cut him down?"

That church strongly considered leaving the hole there and installing a plaque in memory of the occasion. For I did have a far-reaching impact! Those inimitable remembrances will endear you to your parishioners.

Reread this volume. And if you want to become a "sizzling sensation" in the ministry, go thou and do almost exactly the opposite.

Do you happen to recall the feisty little president who was noted for telling reporters and music critics "where to go." A rampant expression in the country was, "Give 'em 'you know where,' Harry!"

But my final admonition to you is: "Give 'em *heaven*, boys!"